A MARKETING         E

TO MASHEED & HARRY —

     TO YOUR HEALTH, WEALTH,
TRUE HAPPINESS ~ AND THE
QUALITY TIME TO ENJOY
ALL THREE. TO LIFE!

          CHEERS,
         — BOBBY

# A MARKETING PLAN

# FOR LIFE

Robert Michael Fried

A PERIGEE BOOK

THE BERKLEY PUBLISHING GROUP
Published by the Penguin Group
Penguin Group (USA) Inc.
375 Hudson Street, New York, New York 10014, USA
Penguin Group (Canada), 10 Alcorn Avenue, Toronto, Ontario M4V 3B2, Canada
(a division of Pearson Penguin Canada Inc.)
Penguin Books Ltd., 80 Strand, London WC2R 0RL, England
Penguin Group Ireland, 25 St. Stephen's Green, Dublin 2, Ireland
(a division of Penguin Books Ltd.)
Penguin Group (Australia), 250 Camberwell Road,
Camberwell, Victoria 3124, Australia
(a division of Pearson Australia Group Pty. Ltd.)
Penguin Books India Pvt. Ltd., 11 Community Centre,
Panchsheel Park, New Delhi—110 017, India
Penguin Group (NZ), Cnr. Airborne and Rosedale Roads,
Albany, Auckland 1310, New Zealand
(a division of Pearson New Zealand Ltd.)
Penguin Books (South Africa) (Pty.) Ltd., 24 Sturdee Avenue, Rosebank,
Johannesburg 2196, South Africa

Penguin Books Ltd., Registered Offices: 80 Strand, London WC2R 0RL, England

This book is an original publication of The Berkley Publishing Group.

Copyright © 2005 by ThirdWind L.L.C.
Cover design by Charles Björklund
Text design by Richard Oriolo

Perigee trade paperback edition: January 2005

LIBRARY OF CONGRESS CATALOGING-IN-PUBLICATION DATA
Fried, Robert, 1945–
    A marketing plan for life / Robert Fried.—1st Perigee pbk. ed.
        p. cm.
    "A Perigee book."
    ISBN 0-399-53065-7
    1. Success. 2. Marketing—Planning—Miscellanea.    I. Title.
BJ1611.2.F69 2005
158.1—dc22

                                                    2004046427

PRINTED IN THE UNITED STATES OF AMERICA

10  9  8  7  6  5  4  3  2  1

In memory of my parents Aggie and Moe who encouraged me to make my dreams a reality.

And to everyone who has the courage to discover and take action on what really matters most.

# Acknowledgments

I'd like to take this opportunity to personally thank all those people who had a positive influence in making this book come alive.

To my trusted business partner and great friend Bob Zeichick, who came up with the original idea for this book—thanks for your creativity and unwavering support. My utmost gratitude goes out to Giselle Shapiro who passionately poured her heart, mind, and soul into researching and proofing the manuscript. It was Giselle who reminded me when things got hectic that I was writing this book with a higher purpose in mind—namely helping others create meaning, happiness, and true success. Many thanks to Wayne Hart who helped me immeasurably in researching and co-writing the business-oriented anecdotes for this book. Much appreciation to my colleague Joel Johnson who made even the most complicated business topics make sense on paper. I'm eternally grateful to my agent

David Hale Smith who believed in this manuscript from the outset and then had the fortitude to sell it to one of the most respected companies in the publishing business.

I'm especially thankful to my talented and insightful editor, Michelle Howry. She was always there with upbeat words of encouragement and a guiding hand. I'll be eternally grateful to Michelle for her remarkable editorial and organizational skills. She has a wonderful way of making a first-time author feel as important as Hemingway. Thanks to publisher John Duff for believing in the original manuscript. I hope this book serves to reward your literary judgment. Kudos to Christel Winkler for chasing me down on overseas business trips to finalize the manuscript.

A special thanks to my good friend and colleague Dr. Dan Baker of the Canyon Ranch Resort in Tucson, Arizona. Your deep insights on life and mentorship will always mean a lot to me. To my highly talented literary publicist Peg Booth and her hardworking associates Kelly Frost and Lane Harden—you ladies are the best in the business. Thanks for believing in me.

My appreciation to Marilyn Bellock who helped me formulate the basic concept of this book and to my ardent supporter Judie Framan who helped me edit the initial proposal. A special vote of thanks to Ken Hoffman whose early read of the manuscript greatly encouraged me. My gratitude goes out to Andy Candelaria for his wonderful creative contribution to this book. A note of appreciation to Don Bowen who put me on his KRML (Carmel-by-the-Sea, CA) talk show a day before we had a book deal signed with the publisher.

I'm ever grateful to my first business mentor Ed Reavey for having the patience to teach me the twelve-point marketing planning process, which serves as the cornerstone of this book. A heartfelt acknowledgment to my lifelong friend Donald Mainwaring for mentoring me in the lessons of life—a formidable task for those of you that know me.

My gratitude to Dr. Peter Koestenbaum whose insightfulness and philosophical brilliance was a key motivating factor in the authorship of this book. To my two trusted advisors Nace Benun and Don Parker, a hearty thanks for helping me balance my life decisions regarding money and meaning.

I'd also like to recognize my brother Dennis for being so supportive and my sister Karen for being the true backbone of our family. Her work in providing dignity and comfort to terminally ill patients is an inspiration to all of us.

In closing, I'd like to commend all of you out there who are on the same journey as myself. A journey of rediscovery. A journey to find life's meaning and true purpose. Your journey won't be easy but when the dust clears, you'll be well on your way to discovering what really matters most.

# Contents

Introduction: What Is a Marketing Plan for Life?                      xi

1   DEFINE THE BUSINESS YOU'RE IN
    Figuring Out Who You Are and Who You Want to Become               1

2   ASSESS THE MARKET
    Capitalizing on Your Strengths                                   13

3   IDENTIFY THE TARGET CUSTOMER
    Discovering the Authentic You                                    27

4   LAUNCH YOUR STRATEGY
    Finding Your Niche—and Daring to Risk                            39

5   WEATHER THE PRODUCT CYCLES
    Reinventing Yourself at Every Stage                              53

6   HIT YOUR FOUR COMMUNICATION KEYS
    Building Your Personal Brand                                     69

7   EXPAND YOUR REACH
    Creating a Legacy                                                81

8   BUILD A HIGH-IMPACT ADVERTISING CAMPAIGN
    Reawakening the Creativity Within You                            93

9   PLAN YOUR DISTRIBUTION
    Sharing Your Time and Energy Wisely                              111

**10   ACHIEVE YOUR SALES GOALS**
Reaching Out to Make Your Personal Goals a Reality          125

**11   ANALYZE THE PROFIT AND LOSS**
Tallying Your Personal Balance Sheet          139

**12   ESTABLISH TARGETS OF OPPORTUNITY**
Making Your Dreams Come True          155


Epilogue          171

# Introduction:
# What Is a Marketing Plan for Life?

*"Success"*
*To laugh often and much;*
*to win the respect of intelligent people*
*and the affection of children;*
*to earn the appreciation of honest critics*
*and endure the betrayal of a false friendship;*
*to appreciate beauty, to find the best in others,*
*to leave the world a bit better, whether by a healthy child*
*or garden patch or a redeemed social condition;*
*to know even one life has breathed easier*
*because you have lived.*
*This is to have succeeded.*
—RALPH WALDO EMERSON

I always thought that Ralph Waldo Emerson had a meaningful handle on success. True success always involves reaching out to people beyond ourselves and searching for a definition of success that's more than a promotion, a title, or a paycheck.

But until a couple of years ago, I was as guilty of this type of narrowly defined success as most Americans. I was a "successful" marketing executive with Fortune 500 clients all over the world. I made a lot of money. I drove a BMW convertible. I lived in an oceanfront home. But I knew something was missing.

Eric Aronson, the author of *Dash,* tells us that on our tombstone there will be two dates . . . our date of birth and the date we died. The dash in between is how we lived our life and the impact we made while on this planet. After taking a step back and realizing a broader, more meaningful concept of success, I decided it wasn't enough to have etched on my tombstone, "sold a lot of stuff."

But how do we learn to achieve the full measure of success, as articulated by Emerson? While pondering this question, I began to realize that the same marketing discipline I had successfully used on a wide range of Fortune 500 and start-up companies could be applied back to our personal lives as well. **In short, the basic principles inherent in any good marketing plan could be reapplied in ways that could lead to a more balanced, fulfilling, and meaningful life.** The same business road map that helped steer companies in the right direction could steer us as well. Accordingly, I believe we should consider developing our personal life plan as if it were a marketing plan for our business. I call this life/work process a Marketing Plan for Life.

In life as well as business, we need to take an inventory every now and then. It has always amazed me that we routinely take our cars in for a six-month checkup, or that we hire a floral service to water our office plants on a regular basis. Yet, many of us let our personal lives go without maintenance. Equally astounding is that couples plan their wedding ceremony and reception for a year, but spend almost no time planning the rest of their lives that they intend to share together. Is it any wonder that our divorce rate is so high?

The premise of this book is profoundly simple: If we take the same amount of time, energy, and focus in planning our personal lives as we do in planning our professional lives, we can live a more balanced, purposeful, and meaningful life. All of this sounds simple. However, making it happen is no easy task. It's not an overnight thing—it's a process. But if you stick with it, the Marketing Plan for Life process will help you discover what really matters most to you.

## Defining Ourselves by Our Careers

Today, even in business circles, it's no longer just about profit—it's also about meaning. Let's face it, throughout the years, many of us cut our teeth in business. It has typically been the way to achieve the American Dream. Our education and well-honed skills were acquired to get ahead and succeed—sometimes at all costs. As we happily leaped through every professional hoop presented to us, is it any wonder that many of us come to define ourselves and our success solely by our careers?

Your career identifies what you do, but not necessarily who you are. Who are you really, at your very core, at your very essence? When you strip away the veneer, are you just a financial planner, a working mother, a clinical psychologist, a teacher, a firefighter, a writer, a marketing executive? Many of us like to believe and live out career labels. But here's one stumbling block: When you live only by your career label, you immediately set up boundaries that limit the ways you can become truly successful. Having a successful career presents only one criteria of success.

The business section of the marketing-plan process originates in part from the Harvard Business School, my former mentor at Motorola, and my own personal school of hard knocks as to what works and doesn't work in the real world. This process has been successfully applied to companies like Motorola, Quasar Electronics, Marantz, Laura Ashley, Eddie Bauer Eyewear, and Nautilus, just to name a few. Believe me, this marketing-plan process works just about every time, whether you're marketing a product or a service. What it doesn't do is guarantee any measure of success in our personal lives. The outline below gives an executive summary of how the Marketing Plan for Life processes works. Subsequent chapters will go through each point separately.

## Twelve-Point Marketing Plan for Life Outline

| MARKETING STATEMENT | | PERSONAL RESTATEMENT |
|---|---|---|
| I. DEFINE THE BUSINESS YOU'RE IN | ⟶ | I. Figure Out Who You Are and Who You Want to Become |
| II. ASSESS THE MARKET | ⟶ | II. Capitalize on Your Strengths |
| III. IDENTIFY THE TARGET CUSTOMER | ⟶ | III. Discover the Authentic You |
| IV. LAUNCH YOUR STRATEGY | ⟶ | IV. Find Your Niche—and Dare to Risk |
| V. WEATHER THE PRODUCT CYCLES | ⟶ | V. Reinvent Yourself at Every Stage |
| VI. HIT YOUR FOUR COMMUNICATION KEYS | ⟶ | VI. Build Your Personal Brand |
| VII. EXPAND YOUR REACH | ⟶ | VII. Create a Legacy |
| VIII. BUILD A HIGH-IMPACT ADVERTISING CAMPAIGN | ⟶ | VIII. Reawaken the Creativity Within You |
| IX. PLAN YOUR DISTRIBUTION | ⟶ | IX. Share Your Time and Energy Wisely |

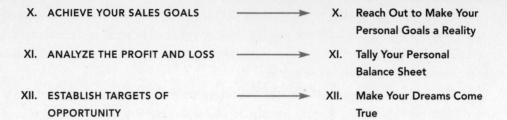

| | | | | |
|---|---|---|---|---|
| X. | ACHIEVE YOUR SALES GOALS | → | X. | Reach Out to Make Your Personal Goals a Reality |
| XI. | ANALYZE THE PROFIT AND LOSS | → | XI. | Tally Your Personal Balance Sheet |
| XII. | ESTABLISH TARGETS OF OPPORTUNITY | → | XII. | Make Your Dreams Come True |

*Be not afraid of going slowly. Be afraid of standing still.*

—CHINESE PROVERB

## Benefits of a Marketing Plan for Life

Now it's time to take ourselves on an exciting journey. A courageous journey. A journey of self-discovery. I'm not just coming along for the ride—I'm taking the entire journey with you. We don't need to have all the answers. The quest or the journey itself is an integral part of the answer.

By the time we finish this book together, you'll be well on your way to developing your own Marketing Plan for Life. A word of caution, however: This plan is a living, breathing document, not something that gathers dust on the bookshelf in your den. Similar to a marketing plan for a business, it needs to be reviewed at least every six months. Just as market conditions constantly change, our personal lives are in a constant state of flux. Revisit your plan. Make sure it remains in alignment with your true purpose or special calling in life.

Nobody said life is easy. Sometimes it's a struggle. But often in the struggle we find meaning. When asked what it was like to be a living legend, longtime Rolling Stones lead guitarist Keith Richards answered, "The legend part is easy. It's the living part that's hard."

# A MARKETING PLAN FOR LIFE

CHAPTER 1

# DEFINE THE BUSINESS YOU'RE IN:
## Figuring Out Who You Are and Who
## You Want to Become

*The purpose of life is a life of purpose.*
—ROBERT BYRNE

The first step in the overall marketing-plan process is to define the business you should be in. Answering this question forces a company to articulate exactly what it does, as well as its raison d'être, or reason for being. It is the first step in establishing the strategic direction for a company.

It's important not to underestimate the importance of this seemingly simple question. For example, if the Pennsylvania Railroad understood that they were in the overall transportation business rather than just the railroad business, perhaps they would be in business today. Pity the poor guy in the early 1900s who clung to the notion that he was in the buggy-whip business when the first Model Ts came onto the scene. Stop and think about it: What business is Calvin Klein in? He said it himself: "I don't design clothes, I design dreams." McDonald's is not really in the hamburger business—it's in the real estate business.

Early in my career, while working with the highly respected Marantz stereo company, I was challenged with a classic case of defining the business for a company. This was an integral part of our turnaround marketing plan to restore the company to its former glory and profitability. After several weeks of research and analysis I defined the business we should be in as "the good-sound business." Simply put, I proclaimed that if our product did not have good sound, we ought not to make the product. When I presented my findings to my brilliant-yet-crusty seventy-year-old CEO, he was less than impressed. "You mean it took you four weeks to write what I already knew?" he asked impatiently. While he readily agreed that "good sound" was indeed the business we should be in, he thought my contribution was basic and unimaginative, especially considering that he was paying me the big bucks. As the spirit of youth would have it, I countered with an explanation. "Well, how's this for imagination? We have nine separate divisions in our company, yet only one division has anything to do with good sound." I strongly suggested that the company sell the other eight divisions that had absolutely nothing to do with the good-sound business and apply the proceeds back to the core good-sound division. My boss beamed and gave me a youthful smile while acknowledging the point. The other divisions were sold, and we succeeded in returning the company back to its former greatness.

> *The great thing in this world is not so much where we stand,*
> *as in what direction we are moving.*
> —OLIVER WENDELL HOLMES

As we would with a business, it's important that we personally define or redefine who we are—and more important, who we'd really like to be. Oftentimes, we have to recognize the disparity or gap between who we are and who we dream of becoming. There may be some accountants out there who dream of becoming world-class chefs. There are a lot of waiters and waitresses who want to be Broadway theater stars. There are lawyers who no longer want to practice law. There are administrative assistants who want to write a screenplay. We have to recognize not only who we are but also who we want to become.

## Constant Redefinition

Motivational speaker Zig Ziglar tells the story of a Cadillac car sales representative from Little Rock, Arkansas, who sold a record number of cars because he defined the business he was in quite differently from the rest of his sales colleagues. "Cadillac Jack," as he was nicknamed, viewed himself as not just a car salesman, but as a "transportation specialist." Accordingly, he offered his customers a variety of services that fit with the way he defined his business. Just a few of the transportation specialist services he offered his customers included the following:

- He picked up the customer's car at their home or place of business whenever the car needed repair.

- He offered the customer free towing service.

- If a customer locked themselves out or lost their keys, he provided a new set of keys.

- He'd jump-start a customer's dead battery free of charge.

- He renewed the customer's auto registration.

Cadillac Jack's record sales came from not only repeat customers, but from a positive whispering campaign that gained him numerous sales leads and referrals. Now there's a guy who truly knows what business he should be in.

Even United Parcel Service (UPS), the venerable package delivery service, has redefined its business. Under the tutelage of CEO Mike Eskew, the company repositioned itself from satisfying customers' small-package needs to synchronizing global commerce. In redefining its business, the company has grown from doing business in twenty-seven states several years ago to doing business in two hundred countries worldwide today. UPS sales have mushroomed from $1 billion to $30 billion—and are growing. "Globalization," said Eskew, "is a whole new exciting business for us. We're challenged every day to do things we haven't done in the past: fly to new places, deal with different governments, and open new trade between countries."

You don't have to be a big company or a hotshot salesperson to redefine your business. My friend Dimitri was a world-class chef and a gregarious restaurant owner. When his restaurant business slowed down, he redefined his business more broadly. Dimitri went from the restaurant-only business to the overall hospitality business. He partnered with a luxury senior citizens' home—offering guests wonderful, nourishing cuisine, warm and comfortable room environments, and imaginative leisure time and travel activities. In doing this, Dimitri not only broadened his business, he heightened his purpose in life. "I love to see the smiles on my guests' faces when I do the little things that really matter for them," he said. "It could be something as simple as giving them a glass of apple juice, long after the kitchen is closed."

Remember, although Dimitri broadened the definition of his business—he still stayed within his core competency. He stayed within the wheelhouse of what he does best—serving excellent food and offering good hospitality.

## Defining Who You Are

We all need to define or redefine our true purpose or "true north" in life. What if Mohandas Gandhi had remained a lawyer and never liberated India? What if Winston Churchill had decided to become a full-time artist, rather than saving Europe from Hitler's tyranny? What if Elvis Presley had decided to remain a truck driver instead of becoming the King of Rock 'n' Roll? What if Abraham Lincoln, a five-time political election loser, gave up on his desire to serve and decided not to run for president of the United States?

All of these now-famous people had a purpose. Once they defined their purpose, they took positive action to fulfill it. We all need to know what our true purpose really is. In her thought-provoking book *I Will Not Die an Unlived Life*, author Dawna Markova explores purpose. "Purpose is the drive to close that circle, finish that song, scratch that itch, bridge that gap; it's the natural energy in each of us—urging growth." Markova urges us to ask ourselves these key questions in exploring our life's purpose:

- What's unfinished for me to experience?

- What's unfinished for me to give?

- What's unfinished for me to learn?

- What's unfinished for me to heal?

Here are some additional questions we should ask ourselves:

- Am I now following a path that leads me to my true purpose in life?

- Am I doing now what I really want to do?

- *Do I even know what I'd really like to do?* (That's the kicker question.)

Don't expect these answers to come in a flash. Exploring your life's purpose is a process. This book will start you on that journey.

## A Life of Purpose

Just as a company has to have its mission or purpose, we as individuals need to find our reason for being. We need to find our true purpose in life. Purpose produces meaning. It helps us discover what truly matters most to us. Purpose provides the answer to the questions, "Why am I here? What is my mission or true calling in life? What is my song? Why was I put on this planet in the first place?"

Rick Warren, in his best-selling book *The Purpose-Driven Life,* explores purpose a bit further: "Without a purpose, life is a motion without a meaning, activity without direction, and events without reason. Without a purpose, life is trivial, petty, and pointless. The greatest tragedy is not death, but a life without purpose."

Sometimes when I struggle with the words I'm writing now, I go back to the very purpose for writing the book: to motivate and encourage people to take action on what really matters most to them. I've convinced myself that I'm not just writing a book: I'm helping people to focus on attaining their goals, dreams, and aspirations. In doing so, maybe, just maybe I'll help myself as well in my own life's journey. For sure, I know I have a need to go beyond just selling more stuff. I'm finally beginning to understand that true success goes way beyond me. I'm beginning to clarify my true purpose. It feels good to have that clarity in my gut and in my heart.

Robert Byrne put it succinctly when he said, "The purpose of life is a life of purpose." But how do we discover our life's purpose? How do we live a life of meaning? These are courageous conversations we need to have with ourselves on the road to discovering what really matters most.

Po Bronson, author of the best-selling book *What Should I Do With My Life?,* says that we all have a true purpose; we just need to work hard to find it because it doesn't always come wrapped as an epiphany. "Purpose doesn't arrive neatly packaged as a destiny," he writes. "We only get but a whisper. A blank, nonspecific urge. This is how it starts." The moment you begin to wonder about finding your true purpose, you're well on your way to discovering it. To be sure, purpose resides somewhere deep within our souls. Coaxing it to come out is no easy task. It takes hard work.

According to author Julie Jordan Scott, one way to know how to define your purpose is to clarify what it is *not*. "Purpose," says Scott, "is not living on automatic pilot; it is not hiding behind the veil of shoulds, woulds, or oughts. Living on purpose is living with laser-like focus. It is responding from an authentic place, deep within the heart. It is aligning with your highest calling, taking a stand for your own truth."

When you live with purpose, you are in essence defining the authentic you—the you you've always wanted to become. Having a purpose allows you to focus like a laser beam on those things that are most important to you. You become very selective as to those things you choose to do and those things you choose not to do.

It's very difficult to have direction in our lives if we cannot define our true purpose or true north. However, once we do find it, we have a sense of where we are going and why.

There's an inspiring scene in the movie *The Rookie,* starring Dennis Quaid, which was based on a true story. Quaid's character is a forty-year-old baseball pitcher who still has dreams of making it to the major leagues, even though he failed in an attempt twenty years earlier. In order to try out again to become a major league pitcher, he has to give up his teaching position—putting a significant strain on his family's finances. Looking for guidance, he goes to his father for advice who tells him, "It's OK to do what you have to do until you figure out what you are meant to do." The rookie made it to the big leagues at age forty.

> *The purpose of life is to be true to yourself.*
> —PO BRONSON

It's obvious that defining your true purpose is not an overnight process, as mentioned earlier; it takes a lot of hard work. (In fact, in a research study, psychologist William Morton asked three thousand respondents the question, "What do I have to live for?" Ninety-four percent responded by saying they had no definite purpose in their lives.) Remember, if you don't know where you're going, any road you take is OK. Carl Sandburg once wrote, "I'm an idealist—I don't know where I'm going but I'm on the way."

But how do you figure out what you are meant to do? Here's an exercise I wrote that was inspired by Cynthia Kersey in her stimulating book *Unstoppable* that might help you define your true purpose in life. The chart won't give you all the answers, but it will be very useful in stimulating your thinking about your purpose in life.

To jump-start you a bit, I've included my answers on the following page:

## Defining Your Purpose (Robert Fried's Answers)

| WHAT IGNITES MY PASSION? | WHAT CAN I DO BEST TO SERVE OTHERS? | WHAT IS MY TRUE PURPOSE IN LIFE? | WHAT ACTION DO I NEED TO TAKE TO REALIZE MY TRUE PURPOSE? |
|---|---|---|---|
| Mentoring others to realize their full potential. | Encourage and motivate people and organizations to realize both their personal and professional goals. | To motivate, encourage, and mentor people and organizations to discover and take action on that which matters most. | Start a new company called ThirdWind that will offer books, seminars, products, and services dedicated to helping people discover and take action on that which matters most. |

Now it's time for you to take a look at exploring your true purpose or reason for being by filling in the chart below. Don't panic if it doesn't come to you right away—it's a process, not just an exercise. By the end of the book, you'll have a far better feel for where you are headed and why.

## Defining Your Purpose (Your Answers)

| WHAT IGNITES MY PASSION? | WHAT CAN I DO BEST TO SERVE OTHERS? | WHAT IS MY TRUE PURPOSE IN LIFE? | WHAT ACTION DO I NEED TO TAKE TO REALIZE MY TRUE PURPOSE? |
|---|---|---|---|
| | | | |

What I especially like about this exercise is that it prevents you from wasting time on those things that are not aligned with your true calling. We're only on this earth for a short while. So pursue things that are in harmony with that which matters most to you. Duke University's head basketball coach Mike Krzyzewski is the epitome of a man who knows what really matters most. He turned down a forty million dollar offer from the Los Angeles Lakers—one of professional sports most storied franchises to stay at Duke to teach basketball, life, and leadership at the collegiate level. When Coach "K" turned down one of the best jobs in all of sports he chose purpose and happiness over money and glamour. "Sometimes in order to be happy," said Krzyzewski, "you have to follow your heart and lead with it." In short, Coach "K" lives what he teaches.

Author Po Bronson puts it into perspective: "The purpose of life is to be true to yourself. To be the authentic you, don't turn your back on your higher purpose."

**One sees clearly only with the heart.**
—ANTOINE DE SAINT-EXUPÉRY

## Igniting Your Passion

While purpose rallies our indomitable spirit and steers us in the right direction, it is passion that provides the fire in our belly to constantly keep us going toward our true calling. Passion is the pilot light that, once ignited, can help us overcome the potholes and boulders that are strewn along life's highway. Passion is what gets us up in the morning to set the world on fire. Dante once proclaimed, "a mighty flame followeth a tiny spark."

Passion moves the heart. In his classic book *The Little Prince*, author Antoine de Saint-Exupéry tells us, "One sees clearly only with the heart." Honoré de Balzac sums up passion with these words: "Passion is the universal humanity. Without it, religion, history, romance, and art would be useless."

When you're truly passionate about what you do, time seems to fly by quickly. You're not constantly watching the clock. You don't mind working extra hours because your passion provides you with sustainable energy. In fact, it is our passion that gives us the energy to deliver the promise of our higher purpose.

I'd like to point out that just because you're naturally good at something doesn't mean you have a passion for it. I know a young parish priest who happens to be an excellent rock-and-roll singer, but that doesn't mean he should give up his true calling to run off and join a rock band.

There's a significant difference between being passionate about something versus being obsessed with something. Passion offers controllable, positive energy, while an obsession is negative and generally uncontrollable. I may love lasagna but that doesn't mean I need to eat five helpings a day. I may love good wine but that doesn't mean I need to become an alcoholic. And with respect to my professional life, while I certainly love my work, I am careful to maintain a sensible work/life balance.

In summary, defining your true calling and real purpose in life is no easy task. In fact, it's hard work. The struggling, however, is a vital sign that you are on a journey toward discovering your true purpose.

We only become truly successful by aligning ourselves with our true purpose and passion in life. When it comes to your true purpose and passion, heed the call. Discover what really matters most to you. Go to your sweet spot and your energy and productivity will soar to heights you've never imagined. When you listen to your true calling, you'll also be a lot happier. I'll tell you what unhappiness is: Unhappiness is not knowing what you want and killing yourself to get it!

## EXECUTIVE SUMMARY

The first step in the overall marketing planning process is to define the business you should be in. Answering this question forces a company to articulate exactly what it does as well as its reason for being. This is the initial step in establishing the strategic direction for a company.

Similar to what a business would do, we as individuals need to define our reason for being. We have to recognize and close the gap between who we are and who we dream of becoming. In short, we need to explore our true calling or purpose in life. Finding our true purpose is no easy task—it's a process. We need to have some courageous conversations with ourselves: Why am I here? What would give my life more meaning?

Defining your purpose focuses you on those things that really matter most to you. Having a purpose tends to ignite our passion. Passion provides the fire in our belly that heads us toward our true calling. Remember the words of Robert Byrne: "The purpose of life is a life of purpose."

I need to mention here that there will be a workbook-type exercise at the end of each chapter of this book. Answering the questions in these exercises may not be easy at first—but don't get discouraged. It's important that you make a personal commitment to complete these exercises to the best of your ability. Remember, you can always come back and revisit your answers after you've digested the entire twelve-points of the Marketing Plan for Life process.

## EXERCISE 1: SELF-DISCOVERY QUESTIONS

It takes some courage to tackle the self-discovery questions in this exercise. However, your written answers will help you define who you are, and more important, who you'd like to become.

### A.  What really matters most?

List the five things, people, or causes that matter most to you. Try to list them in order of importance. (Sample answers are included on the far right to help get you started.)

1. _____ (family)

2. _____ (career)

3. _____ (new career)

4. _____ (community work)

5. _____ (charitable causes)

### B.  What is your purpose?

Utilizing what you learned from the defining your purpose section earlier in chapter one, write a sentence or paragraph describing your life's purpose: (Example: to motivate, encourage, and mentor others to take action on that which really matters most to them.) My purpose in life is:

_____

_____

_____

_____

_____

_____

## C. What are your passions?

List the five true passions in your life. What gives you the most joy? (Sample answers are included on the far right to help get you started.)

1. _____(my young son Michael)

2. _____(the Los Angeles Lakers)

3. _____(cooking a great meal)

4. _____(traveling to Italy's Amalfi coast)

5. _____(breaking 90 in golf)

------

**TIME TO REFLECT**

*Am I currently on a path that will lead me
to my true purpose in life?*

# ASSESS THE MARKET

## Capitalizing on Your Strengths

*He who knows himself is wise.*
—LAO TZU

The market section of the marketing-plan process identifies trends that bode well or ill for your company. Evaluating the market consists of two points: evaluating your own strengths and weaknesses and building upon your strengths. This section will help you to take a snapshot of the market (your life) and allow you to begin the process of finding your company's marketing niche (your personal strengths and advantages). Successful companies use this section of the plan to identify the competition, research the various channels of trade, and measure the vitality of their industry.

Here's an example: In 1995, Levi Strauss came out with a research study claiming that by the year 2000, 80 percent of American white-collar workers would have the option to dress casual every day. Levi's Dockers brand of clothing capitalized on the casual trend—it built upon Levi's strengths (casual wear, denim) and applied them to create office-appropriate casual wear (those ubiquitous khaki pants). Dockers met the surging demand for casual office attire, and Dockers soon became the casual uniform for the everyday man.

This, of course, works on a personal level, as well. My friend Andrew has always harbored a love for the great outdoors. He is an avid fisherman, joyful backpacker and loves to trek the foothills of the world's most majestic mountain ranges. He has always had a passionate concern for protecting the environment. Andrew recognized this was also a concern for all humanity. Harnessing his concern for the environment, Andrew started an eco-backpacking tour company.

His tours not only showcased the beauty of the great outdoors, but also focused on protecting the environment. Andrew capitalized not only on what he loved, but also on his strengths. By doing so, he filled a market niche that could make a difference for future generations.

## Defining Strength

What is a strength? Webster's Universal College Dictionary defines "strength" as "a strong or valuable attribute." But if you make just one meal well, that doesn't necessarily make you a great cook. If you hit one great backhand down the line but can't do it consistently, you're not a great tennis player. So let's try that definition of strength again. A strength is only a strength when you can display your strong attributes on a consistent, day-in, day-out basis. A strength is doing things well, repeatedly, with a sense of passion and joy.

Based on this expanded definition of strength, what is it *you're* consistently good at? What brings you unadulterated passion and joy? What are your strong and valuable assets? What attributes do you consistently display to others? As we'll see in this chapter, when you can identify your strengths and apply them to your work, your chances for success—and your enjoyment of your life—increase dramatically.

## Evaluate Strengths and Weaknesses

When the economy waned in the early 2000s, many companies evaluated their business to stay competitive in the changing marketplace. After riding the casual wave enhanced by the dot-com boom, Levi's sales slumped significantly. A proliferation of new denim brands, discounted products, and khaki pants continued to drive jeans to a mere commodity status. All jeans tended to look alike, and the Levi's brand didn't have the same name-brand cachet it held a few years before.

Recognizing the brand's diminishing sales, the team at Levi's decided to focus on the one key strength of the Levi's brand, one that no other brand possessed—its heritage. Levi's has been around since the gold rush days of 1873. Utilizing the heritage theme, the company created multiple brand extensions, at both the higher and lower end price points. Levi's has treated its brand as a "sanctuary." In fact, Levi's designers frequently research the company's archives to gain design inspiration for new product offerings.

But it's not just your own strengths and weaknesses you need to be concerned about—knowing others' capabilities can give you a leg up, too. Recognizing this, the Oakland A's baseball club built a winning team by utilizing basic business discipline and acumen. The A's religiously measure the strengths and weaknesses of other teams so they can compete on a level playing field—even though they have a player payroll roughly one-third of that of the cash-rich New York Yankees. Oakland's management quickly recognized that they could not compete with teams like the Yankees that spend big bucks to land the major superstars of the day. Because of their financial limitations, the A's, guided by their maverick general manager, Billy Beane, conducted market statistical research that revealed that stolen bases and sacrifice bunts tend to cost more in outs than they pay off in scoring runs. The A's, armed with this research, put a low priority on steals and sacrifices. They've structured their whole team around walks, on-base percentage, and home runs that historically lead to winning ball games. Utilizing their base of knowledge, the A's were able to sign low-cost ballplayers who knew how to get on base and score runs and consequently win a lot of ball games. The A's must be doing something right. As of this writing they have the second-best record in the American League for the past five years, although they've also failed to get over the final hump and win a pennant.

By defining the market and clearly outlining their own strengths and weaknesses, the Oakland A's were able to formulate a strategy to compete on a level playing field with major market baseball clubs.

## Building on Your Key Strengths

Another example of surveying the marketplace and exploiting your strengths against the weaknesses of the competition is Budweiser beer. Budweiser is a mammoth brewer with twelve breweries in the United States alone. Bud also has an extensive wholesaler network that uses temperature-controlled warehouses, strict quality-control standards, and the lowest inventory of the nation's fastest-selling brands. In the 1990s, Budweiser was facing a competitive marketplace getting even more crowded with a tidal wave of smaller, independent microbrew beer makers. The microbreweries boasted handcrafted production techniques and exceptional taste with regional influences. Budweiser's parent company, Anheuser-Busch, had brewery locations all over the world, with a mammoth distribution system to boot. As the very antithesis of a microbrewery, it was arguable that Budweiser could ever compete with microbrews and other beer brands strictly on taste. But Budweiser could go up against anyone on freshness. Budweiser leveraged its key strengths—multiple brewing locations and a sophisticated distribution network—to create its "born-on date" feature. Many beers had pull dates on their product, but this only indicates when the beer is no longer fresh. Budweiser's born-on date, stamped on every bottle, was proof positive of the product's freshness. Freshness really matters for beer and Budweiser communicated this to their customers. And beer drinkers responded. In 2001, Bud Light became the country's top-selling beer.

Recognizing the real trends that lie behind market data is an important part of a company finding its true niche. But clearly, it goes well beyond conventional market studies. Companies need to examine the strengths and weaknesses of both themselves and the competition in order to develop a winning strategy.

## Taking a Personal Snapshot

OK, so we know that to get a good sense of the market, we have to find out our own (and others') strengths and weaknesses and build upon our strengths. But how can we apply this concept to our lives? This involves some honest self-analysis so we can take an overall snapshot of ourselves. We need to initiate a personal "situation review." As Chinese philosopher Lao Tzu said, "He who knows himself is wise." In essence, what we're talking about here is cross-examining and taking personal stock of ourselves. What are your true strengths? What are your weaknesses? Are your strengths aligned with your true passion and goals in life? Remember, it's a strength to know your weaknesses. But it's even a bigger strength to know your strengths. Later, in the workbook section of this chapter you'll have an opportunity to hone in on your specific personal strengths and how you can capitalize on them.

Many of us spend too much time worrying about our weaknesses and not enough time taking advantage of our strengths. We succeed most of the time in life by going to our strengths—not patchwork quilting our weaknesses. In short, we should be accenting the positive, not the negative. We should be less fixated on our faults and more centered on discovering, refining, and honing in on our strengths. Unfortunately, sometimes we take jobs that do not showcase our strengths. In fact, according to Marcus Buckingham and Donald Clifton, in their marvelous book *Now, Discover Your Strengths*, most companies remain startlingly inefficient in capitalizing on the strengths of their people. Utilizing a Gallup database, when asked if they had the opportunity to do what they did best only 20 percent of those polled (out of 1.7 million employees) said yes. But that's not all. Buckingham and Clifton also noted that the longer an employee stays at a company and the higher they go up the corporate ladder—the less likely they are to utilize their true strengths.

*The person born with talent they are meant to use will find their greatest happiness in using it.*
—JOHANN WOLFGANG VON GOETHE

We can't ignore our weaknesses, but we should manage them so we have the time to continue to do what we do best. Legendary football coach Vince Lombardi successfully employed the "go to your strengths" approach with his world-champion Green Bay Packers. Lombardi's players totally bought into his "lead from your strengths" strategy that went something like this: "Men, I want you to know that if we block, we tackle, and we execute the basic fundamentals of our game plan, no team can stop us—even if they know our plays in advance." Under Coach Lombardi's tutelage, his highly motivated team went on to win five league championships and the first two Super Bowls ever played.

Remember, when listing your strengths and weaknesses it's important to go beyond just your job or profession. For instance, if you're a good mother or father, write it down as a strength. If you're a good golfer or tennis player, jot that down. To jump-start you a bit, if a loved one or somebody you respected and admired saw you doing what you do best— what is it you'd be doing? Giving a great marketing presentation? Being a great teacher? Or cooking a great meal? Conversely, if they saw you at your worst—what is it you'd be doing? Perhaps crunching numbers, or trying to cook a great meal! Unfortunately, many of us get stuck doing what we're not passionate about. Go to your strengths—go to your passion. Heed your true calling. Follow your true north. Go to the sound of the bugles!

In his book *Work To Live,* author Joe Robinson suggests we create a new identity card that goes beyond our job, profession, or business title. He urges us to carry an ID card that relates more to how we view our strengths. For instance, Joe Smith: Renaissance Man, Jane Doe: Galloping Gourmet, Ken White: Storyteller Extraordinaire. How would your new ID read?

## Complementary Capabilities

Each of us possesses unique talents and strengths. Our greatest room for personal growth is in cultivating these strengths—not in trying to fix our weaknesses. For instance, in my case, my strength is setting or repositioning the strategic tone and direction for a company. I'm good at steering companies in the right direction. I'm weaker in the area of executing the specific details of the plan. I have a partner, however, who is excellent in executing all aspects of the plan. My partner and I possess "complementary capabilities." All good companies and all good relationships seem to have that needed balance of complementary skills. One person's weakness is covered by another person's strength.

Indeed, in many relationships opposites attract. A shy person who is a good listener may actually feel more comfortable in the company of an outgoing, more extraverted person. The outgoing person may feel more comfortable in the midst of a crowd than they do in a one-on-one situation. These different personality traits are often viewed as positive and complementary.

## Real Strengths

If you want to take full advantage of your strengths, it's important that your strengths are real. You must possess underlying talent to serve as the pillar and foundation of your strengths. For example, you might fancy yourself as a great financier, but you need the skill set and financial aptitude or you're just kidding yourself and others. Superstar Shaquille O'Neal has many talents on the basketball court. Unfortunately, free-throw shooting is not one of them. His career average is just slightly above 50 percent of foul shots made, per attempts. He can practice all he wants, but until he has the proper skill and techniques down pat—foul shooting will never be Shaq's forte. So don't kid yourself, make sure you go to your real strengths—not strengths that serve as false monuments to your good intentions.

*A man should not deny his manifest abilities, for that is to evade his obligations.*
—WILLIAM FEATHER

## Don't Avoid Your Strengths

Believe it or not, some people actually do not utilize their gifts or talents. Sometimes we don't recognize our strengths or attributes for what they are. Sometimes we're afraid to see how our strengths stack up with the competition around us.

My college roommate, Paul, was a shy but brilliant premed student. He was accepted to some of the nation's finest medical schools, including Harvard, Cornell, Yale, and Stanford. His "safety-net school," Vermont, also accepted Paul on that very same day. I took Paul out to the local campus pub to celebrate his scholastic achievement. Over a glass of beer, I toasted Paul and said, "Well, here's to Harvard!" But my roommate flabbergasted me by telling me he had already decided to go to Vermont. A good school for sure, but certainly not as highly acclaimed as the other schools that had already accepted him. I asked Paul why he decided to take the safe route. He responded by saying, "Look, I'm comfortable with the surroundings in Vermont. Besides, I don't need the competitive culture that exists in those Ivy League schools."

I literally grabbed him in the mock choke hold and said, "You're going to Harvard. Harvard needs people like you! If you don't like it, then become an instrument of change." To my delight, Paul reconsidered and went to Harvard. Paul has gone on to become an outstanding pediatrician. Vermont's loss was Harvard's gain.

## Managing Your Weaknesses

Let's talk about our weaknesses for a moment. As mentioned earlier, many of us become absolutely fixated on our weaknesses—but we still need to manage them. First of all, let's try to define weakness. According to Webster's Universal College Dictionary, "weakness" can be defined as "an inadequate, defective quality or trait."

As a boy, I was always very weak in math. Try as I might, I just couldn't seem to grasp anything that had to do with numbers—let alone algebra, formulas, and geometry. Through my sheer ability to memorize (a strength) I somehow pulled through at school in math. But it didn't mask the fact that I had a real weakness that needed to be addressed. Enter Donald, my mentor. He let me know straight away that I probably wouldn't make it as an accountant or vice president of finance. But he felt strongly that I needed to have a better understanding of how money worked—especially since I was about to enter the business world. Accordingly, Donald took me to a series of investment seminars that got me interested in the mechanics of how money worked and investing my money wisely at an early age. He taught me about bonds and the stock market and how to make money by investing over time. In short, Donald taught me how to make money so I could afford to pay somebody else to help me count it.

There are several ways to deal with your weaknesses:

1. Educate yourself about your weaknesses—take a class, read a book, consult with an expert—take training lessons. Don't let a total lack of knowledge make you weak.

2. Find a partner with complementary capabilities who can cover your weaknesses. Often the best partners cover each other—if I'm strong in marketing but weak in finances, an ideal partner for me is somebody who can count! One thing you learn in the army is the person who may not be able to physically take the hill might be the best person to read the map and tell you where the hill is located. That's complementary capabilities at their apex.

3. Ignore your weaknesses and continue to work on your strengths. Why kill yourself trying to do something you don't have the aptitude, skill, or talent for?

## Your Strength Can Be Your Weakness

Sometimes your strength can also be a weakness. For instance, I have worked with some pretty competitive people, and by and large I consider that a strength. But being *too* competitive can sometimes become a weakness.

During our company's annual picnic we had a softball game. Each team was made up of employees of all ages. In fact, the catcher on our team was a sixty-four-year-old grandmother of five. Later, in what most of us thought was just a fun pickup game, our grandmother was literally bowled over by a young, highly competitive twenty-five-year-old man who claimed she was blocking the plate. He scored. She was sent to the hospital in an ambulance. This guy's competitive nature was clearly out of control. His biggest strength (being competitive) was also his biggest weakness.

## Finding Strength in Weakness

Sometimes it works the other way around. Your apparent weakness can become a strength.

A boy who decided to study judo, despite the fact he had lost his left arm in a horrific car accident, began taking judo lessons with an old Japanese master. However, after three months of training the master had only taught the boy one judo move. "Shouldn't I be learning more moves?" the boy inquired of his master. "This is the only move you'll know—but it's the only move you need to know," the sensei replied.

Several months later, the sensei took the boy to his first judo tournament. Amazingly, the boy won his first three matches quite easily on his way to the tournament final. However, in the championship match, he would face an opponent who was bigger, stronger, and faster. In fact, the boy appeared to be overmatched. Concerned the boy might get hurt, the referee was about to stop the match. "No," the sensei insisted, "let him continue." As the match resumed, the boy's opponent made a critical mistake—he dropped his guard. Instantly, the boy used the one move that he was taught and pinned his opponent. The one-armed boy was now the champion of the judo tournament.

On the way home from the match, the boy asked his sensei how he was able to win the tournament with only one move. "You won for two reasons," the sensei responded. "First, you've almost mastered one of the most difficult throws in all of judo, and second, the only known defense for that move is for your opponent to grab your left arm."

In this case, the boy's very weakness turned out to be a strength because he didn't dwell on the loss of his left arm. He let his supposed vulnerability work in his favor. Similarly, we know that Helen Keller was blind but she had the ability to "see" many things more clearly than most of us. Ludwig van Beethoven was deaf but he could "hear" things that other people couldn't and went on to compose some of the greatest classical music of all time.

*Do the things you do great, not what you were never made for.*
—RALPH WALDO EMERSON

## Don't Let Anyone Talk You Out of Your Passion

Don't let other people, especially family members, divert you from going to your strengths and doing what you do best. Whenever I can, I try to mentor people to hone in on their strengths so they can realize their personal goals, dreams, and aspirations.

One day, John, a very prominent lawyer, asked me to see his younger brother, Scott. Scott was a classically trained pianist and a graduate from the famous Julliard School of Music. Although Scott was a great musician, he had trouble making his financial ends meet. Playing the piano even in a swanky Beverly Hills hotel didn't pay enough to support his new and growing family. In fact, Scott's older brother urged me to convince him that he should give up his music and go to law school—just like he did. When I talked to Scott, we talked about his strengths, including his joy and great passion for music. It turns out, he had another strength—he had excellent organizational skills.

I urged Scott to take his joy for music and combine it with his organizational skills to develop community music festivals to heighten people's awareness and appreciation for classical music. Today he is very happy and passionate about organizing classical music festivals and makes excellent money doing what he does best—doing what he loves to do. The point: Don't let other people, especially family members, talk you out of your passion. Remember, heed the call. Go to your strengths—go to the sound of the bugles! If you do your chances of being truly happy will greatly increase.

## Go for Greatness

One of the best ways to realize your goals, dreams, and aspirations in life is to cease dwelling on your weaknesses and to hone in on your positive strengths, attributes, and achievements. You only limit your potential by dwelling on your weaknesses or what you don't do well. We all have greatness within us just waiting to be unleashed on the world. As Ralph Waldo Emerson said, "Do the things you do great, not what you were never made for."

One of life's glorious things is to understand and value our gifts and attributes, and then reapply them positively to others.

As personal coach Rachelle Disbennett-Lee says, "The task of life is to determine what your gifts are and then decide how to use them. We may want to turn our gifts into a profession, or use our gifts in our volunteer work or in a hobby. We don't have to make money with our gifts to have them be of value. Using them to make our lives and others' richer is priceless." I repeat, go to your strengths—go to the sound of the bugles!

## EXECUTIVE SUMMARY

In business, the market section of the planning process recognizes market trends and takes action steps to address them in order to begin the first phase of finding the company's true niche. On the business front, the market section also examines the strengths and weaknesses of the competition.

Just like the market section of the plan, we as individuals need to do some self-analysis and take an overall snapshot of ourselves. We should initiate a personal-situation review. It is very important that we define our personal strengths and weaknesses. However, our major focus should be to capitalize on our strengths and manage around our weaknesses. We excel in life by maximizing our strengths, not by trying to make a patchwork quilt of our weaknesses. So, know and respect your strengths. "Go to the sound of the bugles."

### EXERCISE 1: HONE IN ON YOUR STRENGTHS

Knowing your strengths, put a check mark next to those words that define you best. Then, review the list one more time and cross out those words that are definitely not strengths of yours. Remember, go to your strengths and manage around your weaknesses.

| | | |
|---|---|---|
| __ Acting | __ Doing | __ Initiating |
| __ Budgeting | __ Editing | __ Innovating |
| __ Building | __ Encouraging | __ Leading |
| __ Calibrating | __ Enforcing | __ Managing |
| __ Competing | __ Evaluating | __ Mentoring |
| __ Connecting | __ Executing | __ Monitoring |
| __ Cooking | __ Funding | __ Motivating |
| __ Creating | __ Helping | __ Organizing |
| __ Detailing | __ Imagining | __ Persuading |
| __ Directing | __ Implementing | __ Producing |

| __ Quantifying | __ Serving | __ Tweaking |
| __ Reading | __ Solving | __ Understanding |
| __ Researching | __ Speaking | __ Visualizing |
| __ Risking | __ Strategizing | __ Other |
| __ Selling | __ Teaching | __ Other |

## EXERCISE 2: TAKE A PERSONAL SNAPSHOT

A. Ben Franklin used this simple plus-and-minus chart, which you'll find useful in analyzing your strengths and weaknesses. Utilizing what you gleaned from Exercise 1, fill in your strengths and weaknesses in the chart below. Remember: Do not restrict your strengths and weaknesses to your career. Include your personal traits as well.

### Ye Olde Ben Franklin Chart

| STRENGTHS (+) | WEAKNESSES (–) |
| --- | --- |
| 1. _____ | 1. _____ |
| 2. _____ | 2. _____ |
| 3. _____ | 3. _____ |
| 4. _____ | 4. _____ |
| 5. _____ | 5. _____ |
| 6. _____ | 6. _____ |
| 7. _____ | 7. _____ |
| 8. _____ | 8. _____ |
| 9. _____ | 9. _____ |
| 10. _____ | 10. _____ |

B. After you have completed your chart, ask five people who know you (not just friends or immediate family) to list your top three strengths and weaknesses. Check if their input is similar to your list. Is what you think of yourself the same as how others see you? (for example, if you thought you were a great leader but others don't, you need to narrow the gap between perception and reality?)

## EXERCISE 3: CAPITALIZE ON YOUR STRENGTHS

List the ways in which you can best capitalize on your professional strengths to add joy and meaning to your personal life (for example, if you are a good writer or good speaker, you could use your communications skills to benefit others by writing a column for the community paper or lecture at the local college).

_____

_____

_____

_____

_____

_____

## EXERCISE 4: FROM GOOD TO GREAT

What is it that you can do as good as (or better than) most?

_____

_____

_____

_____

_____

_____

_____

_____

## EXERCISE 5: CREATE YOUR NEW ID CARD

Create a new identity card that goes beyond your job, profession, or business title (for example, Jane Doe: Galloping Gourmet, Eleanor Smith: Designer Extraordinaire).

Name: _____

New ID: _____

## EXERCISE 6: MANAGE YOUR WEAKNESSES

List the ways in which you can best manage around your weaknesses (for example, if I'm good at closing deals, but a poor implementer, I might hire somebody with complementary administrative skills to balance my weaknesses).

_____

_____

_____

_____

_____

_____

_____

### TIME TO REFLECT

*Think about how you can best capitalize on your strengths and manage around your weaknesses.*

# CHAPTER 3

# IDENTIFY THE TARGET CUSTOMER:

## Discovering the Authentic You

*It's never too late to be what you might have been.*
—GEORGE ELIOT

In the Marketing Plan for Life process, the target customer section hones in on who the company is trying to reach with its product or service. Many companies define the target audience based on traditional demographics—gender, age, income, and education. This research helps to narrow down the focus to the most lucrative segment of the market for a company's product or service.

But target-customer profiles also include psychographics—the psyche beyond the numbers. For example, a person can be thirty-five years old but think like they are fifty. A family can make $50,000 per year but spend like they make $150,000. Think about men's cologne. The product is clearly designed for men, but the end customer (purchaser) is frequently a woman, buying the product for the man in her life. When crafting a marketing strategy, men's cologne manufacturers consider targeting not only the end user (probably a man) but also the purchaser (frequently a woman).

One of the best examples of looking beyond traditional demographic data was the introduction of the Ford Mustang. When it first came out in 1964, Ford's Lee Iacocca positioned the Mustang as a sporty, affordable graduation gift for young adults. But what happened in reality was that the dad flipped the keys of his station wagon to his kid and drove off in the sporty Mustang, thinking and feeling twenty-five years younger! Much like the example of men's cologne, Ford marketing executives discovered—after the fact—that their target customer was indeed multifaceted. When identifying a target customer, companies must search deeper, delve into the customer's psyche, and look for the true meaning beyond the numbers.

The combined use of traditional demographics and psychographics is an effective way to construct an authentic profile of a target audience. It also provides direction to product development, communications, advertising, sales, and the rest of the elements of a good marketing plan. Without a clear target-customer profile, a company may waste effort and resources developing products and creating communications to reach people outside the profile. Companies must take care not to stray too far from their core target audience in an effort to extend the reach of their brand. A wide focus targets more people, but speaks to no one, and customers of all kinds will question the authenticity of the watered-down message. A company must take great care in defining its true customer base and know when enough is enough when attempting to extend their brand beyond the initial target focus.

> ### It's not the mountain we conquer—but ourselves.
> —SIR EDMUND HILLARY

On a personal level, the target customer you're trying to reach is the real you—the authentic you. The you at your very core. The you that's left when you strip away the veneer. The you that resonates when you listen to your inner voice. The you that emerges from the pit of your stomach saying, "Hey, this just doesn't feel right—this is not the real me. This is not what I want to be."

But how do you find yourself? How do you set out to discover the real you? How do you capture the true essence of your being? An authentic life is best built from the inside out—by taking a personal inventory. To discover our authenticity we need to ask ourselves these courageous questions: What matters most to me? Who do I need to be to give my life more meaning or purpose? You find your authenticity when you carve out a life that is in harmony with what matters most. When you accomplish this, you are well on the road to unmasking yourself and becoming the authentic person you were always meant to be.

## Authenticity Is Key

Eddie Bauer has long made outdoor-inspired apparel for the casual lifestyle. People familiar with the brand make the distinction between Eddie Bauer and more gear-oriented brands like The North Face with the quip, "If you can die doing it, it's probably not Eddie Bauer." Though designed for less extreme use than some competitors, the brand built its success by proving itself to be an authentic outdoor-apparel brand name with its legitimate link to the outdoor lifestyle. In fact, the company's founder and namesake started an outdoor sporting goods store in Seattle in 1920. An avid outdoorsman, Bauer nearly froze to death while on expedition and the experience inspired him to design a unique goose-down quilted jacket, which he later patented.

Years later, the company maintains a link to this outdoor heritage and has usually paid the consequences when it strayed too far from the brand's authentic roots. In the late 1990s, Eddie Bauer deemphasized the more rugged outdoor roots of the brand and positioned itself against successful casual- and office-attire retailers Banana Republic and J.Crew. As Eddie Bauer's sales slumped, the company realized its mistake and soon re-tuned to the outdoor-inspired casual apparel consistent with the brand's roots. Clearly, the Eddie Bauer target customer appreciates the authenticity of the brand's casual apparel and noticed right away when the focus was altered.

Good companies also understand the importance of authenticity in product and marketing messages when it comes to reaching their target customer. One company actually names their product to reflect its authenticness. Majestic Athletic, a licensed supplier of replica jerseys and merchandise to Major League Baseball and the National Basketball Association, launched a new product line called the MLB Authentic Collection. The Authentic Collection is a line of apparel identical to what is worn on the field by all thirty Major League Baseball clubs, including jackets, jerseys, uniforms, batting jerseys, outerwear, turtlenecks, T-shirts, and fleece. For longtime baseball fans that have endured cheap and substandard facsimile caps and jerseys, Majestic's Authentic Collection is a welcome change. Majestic clearly understands the desire of baseball fans to wear the exact same jerseys and hats that their favorite players wear on the field. The fact that they name the collection Authentic is a powerful gesture of this commitment to their customers. The net result is the company's Authentic Collection has achieved record sales and growth.

*Be who you are and say what you feel, because those who mind don't matter, and those who matter don't mind.*

—DR. SEUSS

## Be True to Yourself

When you live authentically you're being true to yourself because you're living a life that is aligned and in sync with your purpose. Being authentic means you reflect your value system, your true essence—your core beliefs. When you live an authentic life, there is no need to keep up with the next-door neighbor. There's only the need to stay true to yourself and honor your true essence.

Authenticity is staying connected to the truth of who you are—not what others perceive you to be. When I was about to choose a graduate school, my dad wanted me to be a lawyer. I almost went to law school out of sheer respect for my father. But deep down I knew I could only be a good lawyer—never a great one. I thought I'd be great arguing my case in front of a jury but merely OK at doing the nitty-gritty research and paying attention to the details that are required of a great lawyer. I passed on being a lawyer because it just wasn't me.

To discover the real you, you need to be like an archaeologist. You need to dig deep and delve into your own psyche to discover who you are, and importantly, who you are not. According to author Dr. Dwight "Ike" Reighard, in his book *Discovering Your North Star*, "We experience significant stress pretending to be someone we're not. It's like trying to hold balloons under water. We may be able to wrestle one or two beneath the surface, but sooner or later one pops up . . . usually with intensity."

## Sweet Simplicity

Coca-Cola is one of the world's most recognized brand names. But as early as the 1950s, rival Pepsi started to make inroads on the perennial soda beverage king. Pepsi used lower prices and youthful advertising campaigns, but nothing was as effective as the taste issue. In blind tests run by both Pepsi and Coke, consumers consistently preferred the taste of Pepsi basically because Pepsi is much sweeter. At first try, people would get a smoother taste with Pepsi on a sip-by-sip basis. Coke, meanwhile, had never changed its formula in over ninety years of existence. But market research made Coke consider the unthinkable:

change the taste. They did taste tests and ran focus groups, and the findings seemed to support changing the taste. In retrospect they asked their customers every question in the book except the only one they really needed to ask: "If we took away Coca-Cola and gave you New Coke, would you accept it?"

Well, the answer can be found in most marketing textbooks. Consumers made it clear—both vocally and in their actions—that they wanted the original formula, and seventy-seven days later they brought Classic Coke back. Acknowledging the consumers' power in the marketplace, Coke learned that its customers' love of the classic formula went beyond taste—they clearly loved the authenticity of the brand, as well. And as soon as they tinkered with the formula in an effort to expand the appeal, the core target customers rejected the new product immediately. However, by returning to the simpler, original formula, Coke once again became "the real thing." Today, Coke capitalizes on the simplicity, heritage, and "classic" nature of its brand. It learned the hard way that less is often more.

*The ability to simplify means to eliminate the unnecessary so the necessary may speak.*
—HANS HOFFMAN

## Less Is More

In order to connect with our authenticity we might also do well to simplify our lives, not make them more complicated. Remember, a sculptor creates a beautiful statue by chipping away at those parts of the marble stone that are not needed. Maybe we should manage less stuff, not more. Create fewer options—not so many that we fail to exercise any of them. It might do us all well to concentrate less on the things we'd like to acquire and more on who we'd like to become.

Shortly after his wife died, comedian and satirist George Carlin wrote eloquently on the concept of enoughness: "We have multiplied our possessions, but reduced our values. We talk too much, love too seldom, and hate too often. We have learned how to make a living, but not a life. We've added years to our life, not life to our years."

One of the keys to living a fulfilled life—a life centered on purpose—is realizing when enough is enough. In life as well as business, we once again see that less sometimes is more.

## Masking the Real You

Leading toy maker Mattel tried to put on a "different face" in the early 1980s by entering the highly competitive, low-margin, consumer-electronics business with handheld games. The company not only lost money but lost its corporate focus by trying to be something it wasn't. When Mattel did an about-face and refocused on selling its highly profitable collection of Barbie dolls, the company once again prospered.

Let's face it: Most of us are less than honest when it comes to letting people know who we really are. In fact, some of us wear masks pretending to be somebody we're not. In Ancient Greek and Roman theater men wore masks to play different roles, including that of a woman. In fact, the word "hypocrite" comes from the Greek word *hypocrites*, which means actor, one who plays a role, pretends, or wears a mask. Of course, one definition of mask is a device that wholly or partially conceals the face. It is interesting to note that even the word "person" is derived from the Greek word meaning mask or role played by an actor. OK, so where am I taking you with all this? Simple: All of us wear masks at one time or another—pretending to be somebody we're not. Shakespeare said, "God has given you one face and you make yourself another."

When I was a very young man I was once told that I sometimes wore a comical mask to hide my true intensity. Some people wear tough-guy masks to hide their sensitivity. Others wear a brave mask to hide the fact that they are frightened to death. Some people wear the mask of a warrior when in reality they lack the courage to fight for themselves and stand up for what they truly believe. When we mask ourselves we are pretending to be someone we're not. When we wear a mask, we're living a lie—a life of pretense. A life in which the mask you wear hides your true face to the world. Nathaniel Hawthorne wrote in his famous novel *The Scarlet Letter,* "No man for any considerable period can wear one face to himself and another to the multitude without finally getting bewildered as to which may be true."

According to author Bill Treasurer, there are real benefits in living an authentic life: "The benefit of being our authentic selves is that instead of wasting time pretending to be someone we're not, we have more impassioned energy to get on with the business of living. Living a life of authenticity represents the end to an exhausting game of make-believe." What real benefit is there in playing hide-and-seek? We only waste our energy trying to be somebody we're not.

*It is better to be hated for who you are than to be liked for something you are not.*

—ANDRÉ GIDE

This "peekaboo, I see you" mask thing just doesn't cut it. We need to take off our mask and reveal our authentic self to the outside world. To find our true meaning in life we must do more than put on a good face—we must become who we were meant to be. Using a biblical metaphor, it's not so much "I am who I am" but rather, "I am the me I'm meant to be." Gene Mage, president of Soaring Oaks Consulting, puts it all into perspective: "Tragically, too many people wake up one day, look in the mirror, and no longer recognize the person looking back. If you have to give up who you are to get somewhere, perhaps it is not the someplace you really want to go." The point is simple: You don't have to give up who you really are to get where you want to go. Being the real you will get you there sooner because the real you is more aligned with your true purpose in life.

## Personal Enrichment

An integral part of being the real you is being satisfied with what you have. Harriet Rubin, in an article in *Fast Company* magazine, refers to the U.S.A. as the "United States of Anxiety." We're among the best-paid people in the world, the best fed, and among the highest educated. Yet our divorce rates continue to soar, our suicide rates are rising, and experts tell us there's no real correlation between having money and being happy. In fact, research consistently indicates that although the United States ranks among the world's wealthiest nations, we are not even among the leaders when it comes to overall happiness of our population. So, it all comes down to this: It's not about accumulating or consuming more stuff—it's enjoying what we have. It's about living fuller lives. It's not about becoming rich—it's about living a life of personal enrichment.

How do you really know when enough is really enough? Consider the story of Alexander the Great, who visited his good friend and mentor Diogenes after a major victory on the battlefield. When asked what his future plans were, Alexander proclaimed that after he conquered Greece he would go on to conquer Asia Minor and then the entire world. Diogenes then queried, "And then what?" Alexander went on to say that after all the conquering was accomplished, he planned to relax and enjoy himself. To which Diogenes responded, "Why not save yourself a lot of trouble by relaxing and enjoying yourself now?" Obviously, Alexander never really quite got the point. He died two years later at the age of thirty-two—supposedly from malaria caught on the battlefield.

I always thought that once I made a certain amount of money I would be free to let the authentic me out in the open. But I learned like others before me, the more money you make, the more you *need* to make—it's a never-ending cycle. Even if you become a multimillionaire, you're reminded that "money doesn't buy what it used to." In fact, in 2002 there were nearly five million households in America with a net worth of at least $1 million or more. How many of them do you think thought they had enough money?

Many of us are on a monetary treadmill . . . and when it comes to money, we don't know when to get off. The more we have, the more we want. And having more isn't enough—unless someone else has less. University of Southern California economic historian Richard Easterlin describes this dilemma as the "Easterlin Paradox"—according to him, because we judge ourselves in relation to others, any real jump in income makes little difference in how we feel about ourselves. So sometimes, the more we get, the *less* happy we become.

Dr. Dan Baker talks about the concept of enoughness in his book *What Happy People Know*. "At Canyon Ranch, I often hear people talk about hunting—for diamonds, planes, houses, paintings, and boats—but what I really hear beneath the surface of their conversation are people talking about hunting down the big prize that will finally free them from two basic survivalist fears that have haunted people from the Stone Age: the fears of not having enough and of not being enough."

However, when it comes to defining true or authentic wealth, things may be changing for the better. Authors Ed Keller and Jon Berry provide a glimpse of hope when they talk about an emerging, powerful new leadership class of target consumers called the "Influentials." The Influentials are comprised of twenty-one million people whose thoughts, behavior, and lifestyle patterns influence the rest of our country. They are profiled as college-educated, married homeowners with solid jobs. They read a lot, exercise, and tend to be volunteers. The subculture of this influential group is explored by Keller and Berry in their book, *The Influentials: One American in Ten Tells the Other Nine, How to Vote, Where to Eat, and What to Buy*. In their book, some of the most important issues facing these Influentials are "What matters most?" and "Am I being true to myself?" At the bottom of the list were four issues: impressing others, status, wealth, and power. The Influentials are not totally obsessed with keeping up with the Joneses. "When it comes to acquiring stuff," said Barry, "the key criteria is what is going to be engaging and interesting, rather than accumulating badges and status symbols."

Author Margaret Young feels that a lot of us live our lives backward. We try to acquire more money to buy more things so that we'll be happy—when in reality, the process works in reverse. According to Young, "We must first be who we really are in order to have what we want." Antoine de St. Exupéry said, "Perfection is achieved not when there's nothing else to add but when there's nothing left to take away." Our true essence is only revealed when we strip away the veneer and get down to our basic foundation—our true values.

*It's better to be on the lower rung of a ladder you want to be on than to be midway up a ladder you don't.*
—THE OFFICE

## It's Never Too Late to Be Authentic

Think about it: Have you been putting your own dreams on hold to make someone else's dream a reality? Do you use your pending mortgage payments as a reason not to move out on the things that matter most to you? Do you use the emotional security of your kids as an excuse not to become who you were meant to be? Do you wear a mask and pretend to be someone you're not? Don't put the real you on the back burner. You come alive when you let the real you shine through.

Jungian analyst Nathan Schwartz-Salant said, "Some people feel they might have been a different person, a better person, if they had gone another route." Harriet Rubin adds this insight from her article in *Fast Company* magazine, "You feel the need to justify the choices you've made—so you end up wanting to destroy not who you are but who you never became."

Being authentic is clearly a matter of choice. Author Bill Treasurer hits the nail on the head: "The Bible tells us that 'many are called but few are chosen.' I see it differently. I think that *all* are called, but few choose." When you choose to be authentic, you are well on your way to becoming the person you were always meant to be.

In act one, scene three of Shakespeare's *Hamlet,* Lord Polonius uttered his now-famous words "This above all, to thine own self be true." Don't put the real you eternally on hold. Be who you are. Be authentic to your very core and the world will rally around you. When you live an authentic life you can look at yourself in the mirror and say, "Now here's a person worthy of my own respect."

*To be what you are and to become capable of becoming, is the only end in life.*
—ROBERT LOUIS STEVENSON

Being truly authentic essentially comes down to this. The more honest you can be with yourself and others as to who you really are, the more likely you are to create a fulfilling and meaningful life—a life that is in synchronicity and harmony with your true purpose or calling. Author Suzanne Zoglio urges us not to deny our inner truth. "Denying inner truth is like trying to keep the lid on a pressure cooker that has built up too much steam. Try as you will, you can't contain it." If we want to live authentically, we cannot mask who we really are deep down inside our souls.

*We all wear masks and the time comes when we cannot remove them,*
*without removing some of our own skin.*
—ANDRÉ BERTHIAUME

## EXECUTIVE SUMMARY

In the Marketing Plan for Life process, the target customer section hones in on who the company is trying to reach with its product or service. This customer profile deals not only with demographics but also psychographics—namely, the true meaning or authenticity behind the numbers. A company must take great care in defining its true customer and needs to know when "enough is enough" in attempting to extend their brand beyond the initial core-customer focus.

On a personal level, the target consumer you're trying to reach is the real you—the authentic you. Not the you behind the mask, but the you that is aligned with your true calling and purpose. We need to be like archaeologists and dig deep into our psyche to discover who we are and what would give our life more meaning. In order to know who we are it is important to know who we are not and what we need less of in our life. Our lifestyle is chock-full of stuff, but more stuff doesn't seem to make us happier. Shakespeare said it best in his play *Hamlet*: "This above all, to thine own self be true." You can't put the real you on the back burner. When we look in the mirror we want to be able to say, "Now here's a person worthy of my own respect."

## EXERCISE 1: THE AUTHENTIC YOU

A.  Describe the person you always wanted to become. (A person of high moral integrity who helps others in the community? A good father and husband who provides for the well-being of his family?)

_____

_____

_____

_____

B.  Have you ever sold out the Real You by compromising yourself? (Have you ever compromised yourself for a corner office or higher paycheck?)

_____

_____

_____

_____

C.  What masks do you wear at work or at home that prevent people from experiencing the Real You? (The brave mask? The comical mask? The pity-poor-me mask?)

_____

_____

_____

_____

D.  Discovering your authentic self: In discovering the real you, it is sometimes easier to articulate that which is clearly not you. On the chart below, list on the left those things that are clearly not you. You can also list the times and places when you feel least authentic. On the right side, list those things, times, and places where you feel like the real you, the you that shines through.

    Once you've completed this exercise you need to take those action steps to close the gap between who you are and who you were meant to be.

CLEARLY NOT ME                          THE AUTHENTIC ME
_____               _____

_____               _____

_____               _____

_____               _____

_____               _____

_____               _____

_____               _____

_____               _____

_____               _____

_____               _____

## EXERCISE 2: LESS IS MORE

Write down the three things you need to have less of to make your life fuller. (For example, fewer e-mails, fewer distractions, less traffic, less work.)

1. _____

2. _____

3. _____

### TIME TO REFLECT

*Are you currently the person you were meant to be?*

# CHAPTER 4

# LAUNCH YOUR STRATEGY

## Finding Your Niche—and

## Daring to Risk

*It's not enough to stare up the steps. We must step up the stairs.*

—VANCE HAVNER

Strategy is a vitally important element of the overall marketing plan process—it's the part that sets the overall tone and direction of a company. Strategy dictates those action steps that a company needs to take going forward. You can come up with all the bright ideas and exciting dreams you want, but without a strategy to implement them and courage to take the first step, your goals simply won't happen.

When a business addresses strategy, the focus is on three points: a unique competence, a call to action, and a willingness to take the right risk to achieve the results you want. A **unique competence** is something that allows you to stand out from the crowd. Companies like Apple, Nike, and Harley-Davidson are certainly companies that offer a unique corporate personality that allows them to be heard above the noise. The best strategies have a clear **call to action**: a straightforward, simple statement that means something to everyone in the enterprise. And finally, the best strategy in the world is useless if you don't have the guts to take a **risk** and put it into action.

A good example of a good strategy is found with the rental car company Avis, whose "We try harder" approach was understood by everyone in the company—from the person who cleaned the car to the person who sold the rental agreement. The Avis strategy would never have worked unless all facets of the company reached out to actually serve customers better than its number-one competitor—Hertz. Avis had the fortitude to stay the course and proudly proclaim its number-two status in sales while taking over the number-one spot in customer service.

In life as well as business, we need to take our unique competence—namely our strengths—and utilize them to find our personal niche or true purpose in life. As we discussed in chapter one, discovering your personal niche allows you to answer some of life's key questions. Why am I here? What is my mission in life? What drives me? What really matters most?

**In a sense, your life strategy is your personal mission statement of where you want to take your life and what action you need to take to get yourself there.**

In chapter two, you identified your unique competencies. And in chapter three you worked to identify your proper niche—where you want to spend more time and effort, and where you don't want to waste your time. This chapter, then, will help you begin to identify a plan (a strategy) to get you from where you are to where you want to be.

## Unique Competence: Where's the Beef?

The Wendy's hamburger chain developed a strategy in the late 1970s that put it on the map at a time when arguably there was no need for yet another fast-food burger franchise. With the hamburger landscape dominated by McDonald's and Burger King, Wendy's did its market research and found that of the millions and billions of burgers being served by their mammoth competitors, none offered a large beef patty familiar to anyone who was ever old enough to have enjoyed an oversized delicacy at the corner drugstore counter. Recognizing this, Wendy's strategic initiative was to publicize the company's oversize burger that, in fact, exceeded the size of the bun. Wendy's executed this strategy with an advertising campaign that saw an elderly woman—confounded by what is obviously a competitor's diminutive burger—exclaim, "Where's the beef?"

In a nod to the generation that actually consumed large-size burgers at the corner drugstore, the campaign amplified what Wendy's saw so clearly in their market survey (billions of small burgers served) and at the same time promoted their ample-size offering. Wendy's clearly took its unique competence into consideration as it found an open niche for that competence in the crowded burger landscape. But Wendy's did take a risk in terms of timing. In the late 1970s there was a fitness boom under way, and people were redis-covering chicken as the price of beef was going up. Despite the far-from-perfect timing, Wendy's went into action anyway and successfully executed their strategy. Wendy's took the right risk and it paid off handsomely in increased sales and profits.

> *What we think or what we know or what we believe is in the end of very little consequence. The only thing of consequence is what we do.*
> —JOHN RUSKIN

## A Clear Call to Action: There Is No Try

It's not enough just to know where it is you want to go in life. You have to have the courage to act so you can actually get there. It's not good enough just to have a mission in life—you need to be actively engaged. You need to be *on a mission*. You need to be in mo-tion. Writing personal strategy statements that only gather dust in some dark filing cabi-net of our den is not going to cut it here. A strategy is only as good as the implementation. It must be accompanied by action. Eventually, we need to take the leap and have faith that there's a net below to catch us.

Implementing your personal strategy requires a clear call to action. You can't just try to do something. Remember the famous scene in *The Empire Strikes Back*? Luke Skywalker crashes his spacecraft in a swamp. He laments to Yoda, the old Jedi warrior, that he'll never get it out. Yoda suggests to Skywalker that he "will" get the spaceship out, by "feeling the Force." To which Skywalker says, "I'll try." To which Yoda counters with his now-classic lines: "Try not. Do. Or do not. There is no try." It's a fact of life that to get at our true pur-pose to fulfill our personal niche we need to pull the ripcord. We need to act. Nothing will happen without action. Bodhidharma, a sixth-century Zen Master, said, "All know the way, but few actually walk it." Former British prime minster Benjamin Disraeli said, "Ac-tion may not always bring happiness, but there is no happiness without action."

> *We judge ourselves by what we feel capable of doing, while others judge us by what we have already done.*
> —HENRY WADSWORTH LONGFELLOW

How many of us have stayed too long at a job we hated because we didn't have the courage to act? The next thing you know you've frittered away ten good years of your life—just because you didn't have the guts to make a change. American industrialist Andrew Carnegie said, "As I grow older, I pay less attention to what men say. I just watch what they do."

The truth is we're a society plagued with inaction. How many times have you or someone you know felt stuck in a relationship that was going nowhere, but found it more comfortable *not* to do anything about it? How many times have you thought of buying that dream house in the country, but all you did was look and wait for interest rates or prices to drop? How many times have we said to ourselves, *If only I had done this,* or *If only I had done that?* The godfather of computer entertainment, Nolan Bushnell, said, "The critical ingredient in life is getting off our butt and actually doing something. It's as simple as that. A lot of people have ideas, but there are few who decide to do something about them now. Not tomorrow. Not next week. But today. We can't just contemplate doing things. Our achievement in life is in the actual doing. It's what we actually do in life that makes us who we are."

> **To know and not to do is not yet to know.**
> —ZEN SAYING

## Action Speaks Louder Than Words

We've all heard the expression "Action speaks louder than words" or "He's all talk and no action." It's what we actually do that counts in real life. Be a person of action. Put your wheels in motion. After all, what good is a Marketing Plan for Life if you're not going to implement it? The things that separate us from the daydreamers in life are the things we actually do.

Charles de Gaulle once said, "Deliberation is the work of many people. Action of one alone." You may dream of writing a screenplay or becoming a published author. But are you really willing to do the work and take the action steps necessary to get there? Are you willing to pound the keyboard and actually do the writing? People who achieve their goals are not afraid to act.

I have a doctor friend who absolutely has the Midas touch when it comes to investing in real estate. He has a simple real-estate investing strategy—buy the worst house in the most desired wooded or oceanfront area. He's not afraid to pay the going price for his property, knowing that a great location will likely yield high appreciation over time. When asked how he amassed his real-estate fortune, the doctor's answer was profoundly simple: "When I see the right property, I act. While others are still standing on the sidelines, I sign on the dotted line. It's my ability to take action that has allowed me to amass my fortune in real estate."

## Sometimes Taking No Action Is Action

The Tao philosophy teaches us a lot about action. It suggests that we observe the heron standing in the water. The bird only moves when it must; it does not move when stillness is more appropriate. Accordingly, there are times when taking no action is an action in and by itself. When billionaire investor Warren Buffett decided not to buy tech stocks during the tech-buying frenzy of the late 1990s, his very nonaction turned out to be a positive action (especially when tech stocks took a nosedive by March of 2000).

> *You need chaos in your soul to give birth to a dancing star.*
> —FRIEDRICH NIETZSCHE

## Discomfort Leads to Action

Sometimes we need to be taken out of our comfort zone in order to finally act. Since I started writing this book, a series of events have taken place that have catapulted me into action on things I've always wanted to do (but always found a way to put on the back burner). First, my father died, an in-my-face reminder of my own mortality. Then, shortly afterward, I realized that my lucrative marketing position was no longer aligned with my true purpose or calling in life. I was suddenly uncomfortable going to work and living a lie. On top of that, my body was giving me signals that it was time to move on. I now realize that my discomfort caused me to act. My story is still unfolding, but I can already see the epilogue clearly in my mind. I no longer have this pit in the middle of my stomach. I am acting on my true purpose and discovering my true self. Every day is an attempt to heed and harness my own advice.

When it comes to taking action, a lot of us are like dazed deer caught in the headlights. We fear making the wrong choice. We fear taking the risk, so we take no action at all. Bandleader Les Brown once said, "You don't have to be great to get started, but you have to get started to be great." Don't wait to get started on the life you've always envisioned for yourself.

## Taking Risks: Don't Wait for That Perfect Time

The most important element in launching an effective strategy is the implementation. Clearly, nothing gets done without a clarion call to action. But more often than not, action requires a degree of risk. The commonsense point to make here is that prior to formulating a strategic plan to take action, a good measure of due diligence is recommended. This separates recklessness from taking a calculated risk that may spell the difference between business failure and success. But when a company does its due diligence—surveys the marketplace, measures risk—it must pull the ripcord! The emphasis on taking action cannot be overstated. At some point, every company realizes that the absolute perfect time to do something will probably never present itself. Somebody has to *do* something, not just *try* to do something.

Successful companies are not afraid to take risks, but good companies take calculated or right risks—risks that play to their strengths. They take risks that are well within the wheelhouse of their core competency. Great companies understand that the right risk can reap profitable rewards.

## Strategy and Risk Keep Nike on Track

A good strategic statement keeps a company on track and keeps it from straying from its stated purpose. Just a few well-chosen, inspiring words can galvanize an entire company to all pull the same oar in the right direction. Athletic shoe manufacturer Nike had a simple brand strategy that was clearly understood by everyone in the company: "Authentic Athletic Performance." "Authentic" guided the integrity and purity of everything the company executed; nothing was to be contrived. This strategy reached all the way to the models Nike used in their product catalogs: If they were modeling running shoes, their models had better be accomplished track athletes. All products and services associated with Nike were to be athletic, not for leisure use. This strategic directive prevented possibly ill-fated ventures into casual and "sports-inspired" dress shoes. Finally, every Nike product had to exude world-class performance and meet the demands of accomplished athletes. This strategy was often expensive and complex to execute and implement. But it did serve to guide the company and keep it from deviating from its stated niche positioning.

Perhaps the best articulation of this simple strategy was in the Nike advertising slogan, "Just Do It." These three simple words captured the state of mind of a world-class athlete, who wins not only under the bright lights of competition but on dark foggy mornings when the alarm goes off for the day's first workout. "Just Do It" captured the hearts, minds, and souls of the accomplished athlete—and the weekend jogger, for that matter—and was a clarion call to action in executing the company's overall strategic initiative. Nike recognizes that unless a company is willing to take the right risk with its brand, it risks not being the brand of choice in the future. So, Nike just did it.

> *You cannot discover new oceans unless you have the courage to*
> *lose sight of the shore.*
> —DANIEL ABRAHAM

## Don't Wait for that Perfect Time

One of life's real tragedies is our fear of committing to action. How many times have you been on the cusp of a decision and found yourself frozen, waiting for the absolutely perfect time to act. The perfect time never seems to arrive. Authors Ron Rubin and Stuart Avery Gold in their book, *Tiger Heart, Tiger Mind*, address the issue of perfect timing. "We tend to put off action waiting for just the right time and just the right place to act, while the very act of waiting actually pushes desired events away from us. A self-inflicted analysis paralysis."

Sometimes trying to time everything just right can cost us our dreams. I myself have a lot of issues when it comes to trying to time things perfectly. Ever since I visited Big Sur in California as a twenty-year-old, I have always wanted to live there. Located just twenty-six miles south of Carmel, Big Sur is acknowledged as one of the most beautiful spots on earth. It has a rugged coastline beauty that rivals the best of Scotland, with far better weather. Big Sur offers breathtaking ocean views, especially along the famed U.S. Highway 1. It is not uncommon to have the ocean spray kick high off the rocks and throw a light mist over your shoulder. I still haven't been able to fulfill my dream, partly because I've always wanted to wait for the perfect time. A perfect time, which so far has not come. There was always a built-in excuse not to live in the land of my dreams. When interest rates were low, prices seemed too high. When prices were lower, interest rates soared higher. When both were favorably aligned I didn't have enough money. Oh well, it ain't over yet. Stay tuned for other personal developments.

## Taking the Leap

When I was younger, my attitude was always "take the leap." As we get older, however, we tend to lose some of our youthful exuberance. We tend to look at things more cautiously as we age. It's more like "look before you leap." There's an incident that happened to me several years ago that reinforces this very point. When I was just a kid, I loved diving off the fifteen-meter high-dive platform. It never even crossed my mind that I could get hurt. I didn't care much about style points. A perfect swan dive or belly whopper was all the same to me. I dove for the pure joy of it. A strange thing happens, however, when we get older. We lose some of those kid-like, positive qualities that allows us to take risks for the pure exhiliration of it.

One day, shortly after celebrating my thirty-eighth birthday, I was relaxing at an Olympic-size swimming pool when I heard a young mother screaming in distress. Her five-year-old boy had somehow climbed about halfway up a fifteen-meter diving platform and was too frightened to come down. For whatever reason, there was no lifeguard in sight, so I gallantly climbed up the platform and retrieved the boy safely, taking him to his mother. Almost without thinking, I decided to relive my youth and re-climb the steps to the very top of the diving platform. I wanted to take just one more leap off the high dive— just for the fun of it. However, as I was climbing up the last rungs of the ladder, my mind wandered in ways that never happened to me when I was a kid full of youth, vim, and vigor. What if I slipped and fell off the ladder? It's been so long since I did this—what if I broke my neck? Does my life insurance cover this? How much money do I have in my 401k? All these things entered my mind. When I finally got to the top of the platform my knees were shaking because the platform seemed twice as high as when I was a kid. Putting all these negative adult thoughts aside, I decided to take the leap. Notice I said leap. I decided at the last second not to dive off the platform but to hold my nose as I jumped feet first into the water. As I emerged safely from the pool, the young mother and others congratulated me for helping her child. Somehow I didn't feel like much of a hero inside. Instead, I wondered whatever happened to my youthful exuberance. Why did a simple dive I took so many times as a kid suddenly feel like such a big risk?

We can't turn back the clock. We're clearly not the same people we were as kids. Wouldn't it be great to regain some of the spirit of our youth? When we risk, we regain a bit of that fearless, bold, youthful spirit. But when is a risk brave, and when is it simply foolish?

## The Right Risk for You

Here's a key question concerning risk: How do you know when taking a certain risk is right for you? Bill Treasurer, in his insightful book *Right Risk,* tells us that risk is right when it's aligned with our true purpose, values, and passions in life. He suggests that successful people take risks because it completes them in some way. It is directed toward a specific destination. According to Treasurer, "right risks are deliberate, focused, and rich with meaning. Unlike ego-based risks, they transcend the bipolar fields of gain and loss and are instead anchored to a higher purpose. Rather than feed one's ego, right risks strengthen one's character. They are fulfilling not because they are fun and exciting (although they often are), and not because they are materially rewarding (although they can be), but because they transport us from where we are to where we ought to be." Taking a right risk will help you close the gap between who you are and who you dream of becoming.

*It's not because things are difficult, we do not dare.*
*It is because we do not dare that things are difficult.*
—SENECA

Make no mistake about it—it takes courage to take a risk. When we risk, we often act in spite of our fear. If we set out to start a new business, we risk failure. If we reach out to love someone, we take the risk of not being loved in return. If we ask somebody out for a date, we risk rejection. When we give a party, we take the risk that our invited guests might not even show up. When we expose our true feelings, we risk being exposed. Anyway, you get the picture.

Life is full of risks, but the greatest rewards go to those who take them. One of life's great tragedies is to risk nothing and gain nothing. We've all heard the expression, "Nothing ventured, nothing gained." Years from now, you don't want to look back on an unfulfilled life and say, "If only I would have taken more risks." As Bill Treasurer says, "Many a bar stool has been warmed by the seat of a man whose taunting recollections are the risks he didn't take." Even though it takes a lot of courage and guts, the great humorist Will Rogers urges us to take the risks in life: "Why not go out on the limb—that's where the fruit is." If we don't take risks we lessen the risk of getting hurt, but we never really live life to the fullest either. When it comes to risk taking, it's William Wallace's voice that firmly echoes in our ear: "Every man dies, but not every man lives."

# EXECUTIVE SUMMARY

In business, a successful strategy offers a clarion call to action. But an action strategy often requires a certain degree of risk. Once a company completes its market research with due diligence, it's time to pull the ripcord.

In a sense, our own life strategy is a mission statement. But it's not good enough to just have a mission. We need to act. Any strategy is only as good as the implementation. We need to take the action steps necessary to make things happen. Often, our action strategy requires that we take risks. The key is to take the right risk for us—the risks that transport us to where we ought to be. It often takes courage to take the right risk. If we don't take risks, we lessen our chances of getting hurt, but we never really live life to the fullest. If we don't act on life, life has its own way of acting on us.

## EXERCISE 1: TAKING ACTION

A. List three times in your life that you regret you didn't pull the ripcord and take action (for example, changing jobs, buying a vacation home, dissolving a bad relationship, etc.).

1. _____

_____

2. _____

_____

3. _____

_____

B. Now it's time we revisit your true purpose or calling in life. Take a look at your earlier answers in defining your purpose in the workbook exercise of chapter one (see page 10, section 1B). Has your true purpose changed since chapter one? Try rewriting your purpose below. Rewrite a sentence or paragraph describing your life's purpose (for example: to motivate, encourage, and mentor others to take action on that which matters most to them).

My purpose in life is:

_____

_____

_____

_____

_____

C. Taking action on your purpose. List three action steps you can take now in order to better position yourself toward your true purpose in life (for example: more quality time with my family, begin to write my screenplay, contribute more to my community and its charitable works).

1. _____

   _____

2. _____

   _____

3. _____

   _____

D. Name three times in your life when your actions spoke louder than words.

1. _____

   _____

2. _____

   _____

3. _____

   _____

## EXERCISE 2: PERFECT TIMING

List the instances in your life when you let things get away because you tried to time things too perfectly (for example, the dream house that got away, the job you didn't take).

_____

_____

_____

_____

_____

_____

_____

_____

## EXERCISE 3: RISK TAKING

A. List the three times in your life when you wish you had taken a greater risk.

1. _____

   _____

2. _____

   _____

3. _____

   _____

B.  What was the result or outcome of not taking that risk?

_____

_____

_____

_____

C.  What were the three best risks you have ever taken in your life?

1.  _____

    _____

2.  _____

    _____

3.  _____

    _____

D.  What was the positive result or outcome of having taken those risks?

_____

_____

_____

_____

_____

_____

_____

_____

E.  What risks do you need to take over the next few months to be
    more aligned with your true purpose in life?

    _____

    _____

    _____

    _____

F.  Risk taker versus risk avoider: Looking back on your life, list the ar-
    eas in which you are a risk taker (for example, investing in stocks,
    gambling). Then list the areas in which you are a risk avoider (for ex-
    ample, relationships, reluctance to change jobs, etc.).

    **Risk Taker**

    _____

    _____

    _____

    _____

    **Risk Avoider**

    _____

    _____

    _____

    _____

TIME TO REFLECT

*When was the last time you risked failure for something
you passionately believed in?*

# CHAPTER 5

# WEATHER THE PRODUCT CYCLES

## Reinventing Yourself at Every Stage

*We live life going forward, but we understand it looking backward.*
—SØREN KIERKEGAARD

The next section of the marketing-plan process involves developing the product—defining what product or service is really needed, and then developing a product or service that meets these real, genuine human needs.

The most important part of successfully meeting these human needs over an extended period of time is the layering-on concept. Investors by and large do not want to invest in a "one-hit wonder." They'd like to know that a company has several layers of product in development that could make that company profitable for many years to come, and that the company is nimble enough to change and reinvent itself to keep up with the current trends. Drug companies are good examples of reinvention. A pharmaceutical company like Merck needs to continually develop new prescription drug offerings, because even their most successful proprietary products will eventually become generic products. Companies need to continually reimagine and reinvent their products to keep their vitality ongoing for the years to come.

*Each age is a dream that is dying, or one that is coming to birth.*
—ARTHUR O'SHAUGHNESSY

Similar to the product layering-on process, each of us is constantly reinventing ourselves. Just as a company has to have definitive "product cycles," we as individuals have "life cycles." We have to constantly redefine or reinvent ourselves as we go through life's passages. This transformation takes place in several ways. We could be changing our career path. We could be altering our lifestyles. In some cases we might even be changing the way people perceive us. The English poet Arthur O'Shaughnessy once said, "Each age is a dream that is dying, or one that is coming to birth."

People, like companies, are in a constant state of evolution. The very fact that you picked up this book indicates that you feel an urge for change in your life. The road to rediscovery is an ongoing process. Part of this process is the need to redefine or reinvent ourselves—not just once, but as many times as needed as we go through the cycles of life.

## Companies Reinvent Themselves

Companies certainly need to layer on new products and services, effectively reinventing themselves and their brand names in the eyes of the consumer. But sometimes companies need to update their logos as well. Purists maintain that a company's logo is sacrosanct—with rigid guidelines for its use, placement, and color—and any change is both rare and momentous. But an increasing number of companies are realizing that redesigning their logos is just as important as redesigning and improving products and marketing plans. Coach is an example of this. Founded in 1941, the Coach brand had always been renowned for quality and durability of its leather products. But by the mid-1990s, Coach was losing market share to trendy upstarts like Kate Spade.

In 1996, the company's CEO and lead designer redesigned the logo with a nod to the brand's heritage and came up with a new signature "C" logo inspired by a piece of vintage Coach literature. Based on its increased sales, the modification was a smash success. Consistent with the product cycle concept, Coach realized that it must continue to improve and update the logo while remaining branded and recognizable. In the case of Coach, the process of reinventing the most recognizable symbol of the company has paid off because it communicates "newness" while acting as a potent symbol of the brand's commitment to design innovation.

Even cities reinvent themselves. The city of Las Vegas is in a constant state of reinventing itself in reaction to competitors and changing consumer demands. Las Vegas began as a gambling oasis in the middle of the Nevada desert. Soon after the 1940s, the city continued to offer gambling with an increasing number of headline acts and bargain accommodations to lure people to the desert. Still later, the city positioned itself as a family destination offering something for everyone in the family: gambling for mom and dad, and plenty of diversions for the kids (think Circus Circus and Treasure Island). Facing eastern competition and increased migration westward, a true building boom and renovation commenced in the 1990s. The new Las Vegas offered huge sprawling hotels, faithfully built around bigger-than-life themes like New York City, Paris, Venice, and the Egyptian pyramids. Once renowned for bargain room rates subsidized by casinos, Las Vegas now offers luxury accommodations, gourmet dining, fine shopping around the clock, and top entertainment. In a natural extension of its move to luxury and spectacle—and partly fueled by nostalgia for the excesses of the Rat Pack era—Las Vegas today appeals to the inherent need to make a spectacle of one's self. Stylish nightclubs and plenty of adult entertainment compete with the casinos and other attractions for attention and tourist dollars. Now more than ever, the house rule in Las Vegas is that as long as you don't bother the other customers, you can do just about anything you want and be whoever you want to be.

At every point in its evolution, Las Vegas has skillfully reinvented itself, altering its strategy and product offerings in reaction to market forces and consumer trends. So, whether it's the boom of amusement parks, casinos in Atlantic City, casinos on Native American reservations, a boom economy, a bust economy, or nostalgia for a bygone era, Las Vegas remains light on its feet and somehow always succeeds in giving customers what they want.

Another great example of constant reinvention is Apple Computer. The company arguably invented the personal computer, not only making desktop-size processors that the masses could afford but also making the computer fashionable through great design. This point of difference has guided the company ever since—whether it is a new line of desktop units in different colors with great new processing features or an entirely new type of product that makes people fall in love with technology all over again. The iPod portable MP3 player is a masterpiece in design and function and has been embraced by the Apple faithful and the recently converted.

Companies clearly need to layer on new products and occasionally reinvent themselves to stay in front of their customers. But it is important for these companies to remain within their core competencies affirmed in Define the Business You're In Section, which is step one of the planning process. This constant movement is also a survival technique, since the marketplace is in a constant state of change year in and year out.

*No man steps in the same river twice,*
*for it's not the same river and he's not the same man.*
—HERACLITUS

## Reinventing Yourself

An amazing example of personal reinvention can be seen by following the storied career of Arnold Schwarzenegger and his ability to constantly transform himself. Arnold came to the United States virtually penniless in 1968. He parlayed his Mr. Universe bodybuilding title into a role in the documentary film *Pumping Iron*. From there, he became Hollywood's highest-grossing action hero, demanding in the neighborhood of $14 million per film. Then Arnold reinvented himself again by layering on humor and sensitivity to his acting skills. This allowed him to take a comic turn in movies like *Twins* opposite Danny DeVito and *Kindergarten Cop*—in which he made fun of his Austrian accent and displayed a gentler, more sensitive side than his previous Terminator-esque roles would have suggested.

Arnold governed his own life with a brick-by-brick construction approach that allowed him to transform his career. Recently, Schwarzenegger has redefined himself once again—from aging action hero to governor of the State of California, the world's fifth-largest economy. What's next for Arnold? Only time will tell. Love him or hate him, his powers of reinvention are awe inspiring.

*Time is a dressmaker specializing in alterations.*
—FAITH BALDWIN

Here are just a few recognizable people who reinvented themselves by altering their careers, lifestyles, and in some cases, their values over time.

**Ronald Reagan**—went from making B movies to become president of the United States.

**John Glenn**—evolved from one of our earliest astronauts to senator of Ohio, and back again as the oldest astronaut to travel in space.

**Tony Bennett**—with aid of his son, who manages his career, he transformed himself from aging superstar singer to hip Grammy Award winner, whose popularity now extends to young people in their twenties and thirties.

**Hillary Clinton**—went from the beleaguered wife of a president to senator of New York to a prime candidate for president in her own right.

**Dwight D. Eisenhower**—went from the commander of our allied forces to president of prestigious Columbia University to president of the United States.

**Kevin Costner**—evolved from a sexy film star to a determined and talented Academy Award–winning director for his movie *Dances with Wolves*.

**Joe Gibbs**—went from a Super Bowl–winning football coach with the Washington Redskins to owner of NASCAR Championship racing cars and back again to NFL coach.

**Madonna**—literally transforms her look and trendsetting music/video performances every couple of years. Her children's book *The English Roses* hit the *New York Times* best-seller list. Madonna is the epitome of a superstar who understands the importance of reinventing herself to stay on top.

My dear friend Walter is the epitome of a person who has totally reinvented himself. At one time, Walter was one of the top personal-injury lawyers in town. Then one morning the police arrived at his home, handcuffed him, and drove him away in a squad car. Walter was booked and charged with insurance fraud and filing false income-tax returns. He was forced to resign from the California bar and slapped with a five-year prison sentence.

While in prison, Walter started to study psychology through a correspondence course. During his confinement, he learned that his young grandson had been diagnosed with autism, a serious lifelong developmental disorder. Walter became interested in securing special educational programs and rights for disabled children, and once he was out on parole, his interest in helping disabled children with their special educational needs began to escalate. He formed a new nonprofit corporation called Professional Advocates for Special Students, or P.A.S.S. The company is dedicated to helping disabled children receive their special educational needs.

Over the past couple of years, Walter has received literally hundreds of letters from thankful parents of specially challenged children whom he has helped. Today, Walter is a widely recognized expert in the field of special education, often assisting others without compensation.

Recognizing that he has reinvented himself toward a higher purpose, the State of California has reinstated Walter to the bar. My Irish mother had an expression for people like Walter: "Never judge a sailor on a calm sea." Walter has survived the choppy waters of life. He has redefined himself. The world of special education is now in a safer harbor because of his unselfish work.

> *Because things are the way they are, things will not stay the way they are.*
> —BERTOLT BRECHT

## Winds of Life

All of us go through various stages or passages in life. These passages could easily be represented in metaphor by the Three Winds of Life:

### First Wind: Dedication and Adventure

This is the dedication and adventure stage. You'll do anything it takes to get ahead. You'll even go for coffee and doughnuts if you have to! If you're like me, you might move five times in this period and never think twice about it. You're not averse to taking risks. Life is an exciting adventure.

### Second Wind: Making Your Mark

Here you've reached a certain level of success and begin to make your mark. But attached to success comes a cost. Under the guise of convincing yourself that you're sacrificing for the overall good of the family, you begin to miss those little things in life that in retrospect aren't so little after all. You miss your son's Little League game, your daughter's soccer match, and that family vacation that you promised your wife you'd take. You've been promoted at work. Now you have more money but far less time to enjoy it. You begin to wonder, "If I'm so successful, how come I'm not happier?"

### Third Wind: Discovery

You begin to recognize that what you do is not necessarily who you are. By this time you might have experienced a failed marriage, an unfulfilled career, or the sadness and realization of your own mortality from the loss of a parent. You begin to seriously question your own legacy or purpose in life. Having a life of meaning now becomes a priority. You're beginning to discover what really matters most to you. And when you do the wind will be at your back.

The Three Winds of Life are not necessarily linked to age. You can experience defining moments in your life that thrust you into a different wind beyond your age. Take tennis star Jennifer Capriati for instance. At age fifteen, she was the number-two ranked women's tennis player in the world. Two years later, after arrests for shoplifting and drug possession, she fell to a ranking of two hundred twenty in the world.

Jennifer then made an incredible comeback. After her second dramatic win in the Australian Open, an enterprising reporter asked her about getting a second wind—to which she responded, "Heck, no, I got my third wind" (and we all know she wasn't just talking about tennis!).

## Defining Moments

Each of life's stages or winds, as we described earlier, are accompanied by defining moments in time that often become turning points in our lives. A good way to understand the changes you go through is to examine the defining moments of your life by each decade of your existence. This isn't an easy task. However, when done thoroughly, it will help you clarify your goals, dreams, and aspirations going forward. You'll be able to see turning points and key moments in your life that will have a significant impact on the way you choose to live your life going forward. The way you respond to these events will shape how you feel about yourself, who you are, and who you want to become. Author Ike Reighard in his book *Discovering Your North Star* said, "Our lives are like tapestries, we can look at the back and see a mess of dangling strings, but when we look at the front we see a wonderful design that God is weaving."

To jump-start you a bit, here's the decade's exercise that I completed on my own life. For the next several pages, I'll be unveiling myself in front of you in a way I've never done before:

### Decade One (1–10 Years Old)

- Hit by a car. I was never supposed to walk again.
- Private tutor schooling. I get all the attention (I still crave it).

- My dad's landmark restaurant is booming (good news). He spends a lot of time at the restaurant (bad news).

## Decade Two (11–20 Years Old)

- Major hip surgery allows me to walk again (albeit with a limp).

- Get game-winning hit in Little League all-star game. My doctor is very proud.

- Begin high school.

- Discover girls.

- Accepted to college in New England. I make dean's list, but recognize that there are much smarter people in the world than me.

## Perspective: Decades One and Two

Looking back on my own life, decades one and two had a lot to do with perseverance and not giving in to the likely prospect of never walking again. But a few defining moments clearly pop into my head:

When I was nine years old I was hit by a car. I had a mangled left hip and was told I would never walk again. My mother and father took me to some of the finest orthopedic surgeons, but all of them refused to operate claiming the situation was hopeless. Then one day we visited the head of orthopedic surgery for the New York Knicks basketball team. His name was Dr. Yanagisawa. The doctor told me I had a fifty-fifty chance of ever walking again if he operated on me. I told him I'd like to take that chance. My mom and dad agreed. After a successful operation, I was walking again (albeit with a severe limp which I was told I'd probably have to live with for the rest of my life).

A year later, I made the Little League all-star team, which made my doctor extremely proud. And then it happened—playing against the previous year's Little League state champions, I drove in the winning run in the last inning with a base-clearing double. I was mobbed by my fellow teammates. I knew I had done something great because our coaches took us later for a celebratory pizza with all the toppings (a clear sign of achievement if ever there was one).

The game was well covered by local press. I couldn't wait to read the story of our victory and my game-winning hit. I got up really early the next day and read the headline coverage of the game, which read: "Limping Boy's Hit Wins Ballgame!" I defiantly strode into the local press office and demanded to see the sports editor. I threw the sports section in his embarrassed face, vowing never to limp again. From that day forward, almost miraculously my limp disappeared. Now when people around me tell me they can't do something I always think of that game-winning hit and the limp that was literally willed away.

## Decade Three (21–30 Years Old)

- Receive master's degree. Write thesis titled "Host City Marketing for the Olympic Games."

- Stint as U.S. Army second lieutenant.

- Start my marketing career at Motorola. Meet my marketing mentor who teaches me the Twelve-Point Marketing Plan Discipline.

- Meet my life mentor, Donald.

- Visit Carmel/Big Sur, California, area for the first time; vow to live there someday.

## Perspective: Decade Three

Looking back on decade three, a key turning point in my life came at Motorola when I wasn't afraid to take a risk. Let me explain.

One day Ed, my Harvard-Business-School-educated boss, called me into his office with an open invitation. He wanted me to come to his beautiful farm in the rolling hills of Barrington, Illinois, to see if I could master his famous Twelve-Point Marketing Plan discipline. That's right, the same discipline that provides the foundation of this book. There was only one catch to my boss's invitation. If he felt that I couldn't grasp or have the aptitude for his marketing-plan process, he was going to "fire me on the spot." I remember asking Ed if I was his first invitee. He informed me that there had been four other "marketing impostors" who had preceded me—none of whom made the cut. None of whom were still with the firm.

As it happened, it was a magical weekend. I was enthralled with Ed's marketing-plan process, and according to my boss, I showed a strong aptitude for capturing the essence of his process. After several months, Ed was so delighted with my progress that he sent me to Motorola Canada in Toronto to implement the plan in our international division. Once in a while, you're in the right place at the right time. Our sales at Motorola Canada tripled and my career and salary skyrocketed.

### Decade Four (31–40 Years Old)

- Work for corporate conglomerate in Indiana. Learn to appreciate Midwest values.

- Move to Los Angeles for bigger bucks to work for a consumer electronics company. My core values are severely tested.

- Meet my eventual business partner.

- Turn around a California consumer electronics firm. Named one of top marketing executives under forty by an industry business magazine.

- My partner and I start up our own marketing consulting firm that becomes very successful (if you define success only as making money—which is what this book challenges).

- We begin to explore the idea to start ThirdWind, a company that would help people discover and take action on that which really matters most to them.

- Instead, we put ThirdWind on hold and take over the management reins of a major fitness-equipment company. Once again, we sell out for the big bucks (I'm beginning to see a disturbing pattern here).

### Perspective: Decade Four

As I look back on decade four, I detect a disturbing pattern—a pattern that manifests itself with many people in their early forties. We lose perspective—our work becomes our life—while often, more important things are shifted to the back burner. As we move up the ladder of "success" we make money, but not necessarily meaning. We wonder, if we're so successful, how come we're not happier? In my own case, I always wanted to have kids, but time just seemed to slip by. I begin to reassess things. I begin to revisit the dreams of my youth. I know that the greatest opportunity for self-discovery still awaits me.

### Decade Five (41–50 Years Old)

- I launch several successful companies.

- I love kids—but I still don't have any of my own.

- Stock market booms, then busts (lessons learned).

- My parents die. I feel lost without them and need to reexamine my own life and how I want to live it beyond work.

- We begin to move our ideas for ThirdWind forward, with seminars, radio interviews, etc.

- I'm asked to write a book called *A Marketing Plan for Life*.

- Still yearning to move to Carmel/Big Sur.

### Perspective: Decade Five

The turning point in decade five was the loss of both of my parents. Your perspective on life changes when your parents are gone. You begin to realize that life on this planet is short and that you won't be here forever. You come in touch with your own mortality. You reassess things. You wonder if you are on course to realize the goals, dreams, and aspirations of your youth. You ask yourself, has my life made a difference to others? If I died tomorrow, what would be my legacy? And it's here that many of us begin a wonderful journey to discover and take action on what really matters most.

> *It's not the events in your life that determine who you are,*
> *it's how you choose to respond to them.*
> —VICTOR FRANKL

### Looking Back/Going Forward

As I look back on my own personal decades' experiences, I take solace in the perspective offered by author Victor Frankl: "It's not the events in your life that determine who you are, it's how you choose to respond to them."

Once there were two brothers. A man asked the oldest brother why he smoked. He answered, "I smoke because when I was young my mother smoked." The youngest brother was asked the reverse question, "Why don't you smoke?" His answer: "I don't smoke because when I was young my mother smoked."

Frankl was right: It's not what happens to us—it's how we choose to respond to what happens to us that shapes us and determines who we really are. Frankl counsels us to roll with the punches. "When we are no longer able to change a situation, we are challenged to change ourselves."

*Nothing is written in stone—not even what has already happened.*

—DR. DAN BAKER

## Our Story Is Still Unfolding

Life throws us some knuckleballs. We really don't know if an event or defining moment is good or bad until we look back in retrospect. How did it shape us? Did it make us a better person? Did we crumble under its weight or did it only give us more determination? As long as we have life, the story is still unfolding.

In an article in *Psychology Today*, Maryanne Garry and Devon Polaschek talk about the importance of our past in gaining perspective on our future: "The autobiographical memories that tell a story of our lives are always undergoing revision—precisely because our sense of self is too. We are continually extracting new information from old experiences and filling gaps in ways that serve some current demand." Consciously or unconsciously we use information from the past to reinvent our present or future.

Personal reinvention is the action that occurs when we adapt to life's changes, turning points, defining moments, or just process in new information that affects our lives. Philosopher Søren Kierkegaard adds this sound perspective: "We live life going forward, but we understand it looking backward." By drawing from the past, we can better understand our future. As long as we have life, our life story is still unfolding.

## EXECUTIVE SUMMARY

The product chapter introduces the product "layering-on" process and the need for all good companies to consistently redefine or reinvent their products and services. It is underscored by the fact that on a personal level, each of us goes through various stages or winds in our ever-changing lives. Just as a company has product cycles, we have life cycles. We have to constantly redefine or reinvent ourselves as we go through life's passages. The defining moments in our life deeply affect our ability to realize our goals, dreams, and aspirations. By drawing from the past, we can better understand our future. As long as we have life, our life story is still unfolding.

## EXERCISE 1: DEFINING MOMENTS BY DECADES

A. Write down the defining moments in your life by each decade since you were born.

Decade One: (1–10 Years Old)

_____

_____

_____

Decade Two: (11–20 Years Old)

_____

_____

_____

Decade Three: (21–30 Years Old)

_____

_____

_____

Decade Four: (31–40 Years Old)

_____

_____

_____

Decade Five: (41–50 Years Old)

_____

_____

_____

**Decade Six: (51–60 Years Old)**

_____

_____

_____

**Decade Seven: (61–70 Years Old)**

_____

_____

_____

**Other Decades (If Applicable)**

_____

_____

_____

B.  Take a step back and review how life's defining moments helped shape or strengthen your character traits. (Making a dramatic recovery from a car accident taught me how to persevere. Getting good grades in school gave me confidence to pursue higher education. Losing my parents helped me cope with tragedy and sorrow.)

_____

_____

_____

C.  Looking back, which decade has given you the most joy? Why?

_____

_____

_____

D.  Looking back, which decade has given you the most regrets or sadness? Why?

_____

_____

_____

E.   What historical or world-shaping occurrence or event has affected your life most? Why?
    (For example, 9/11, Vietnam War, terrorist acts, stock market boom/bust, technological
    revolution.)

    _____

    _____

    _____


## EXERCISE 2: REINVENTING YOURSELF

A.   List the time(s) in your life that you have reinvented or redefined yourself to better
    achieve your goals, dreams, and aspirations.

    _____

    _____

    _____


B.   If you could make one change in yourself or your life today, what would it be? What is
    stopping you from making that change?

    _____

    _____

    _____


### TIME TO REFLECT

*When was the last time you reinvented yourself to bet-
ter realize your goals, dreams, and aspirations?*

# CHAPTER 6

# HIT YOUR FOUR COMMUNICATION KEYS:

## Building Your Personal Brand

*In the whole of recorded history, there will never be another such as you. Each of us is a miracle in uniqueness.*

—PABLO CASALS

The sixth section of the Twelve-Point Marketing Plan process discusses communication keys—how your company can flaunt its uniqueness and separate itself from its pack of competitors. The communication keys serve as a litmus test to determine whether a company has a good chance to successfully build its corporate brand over time.

Just as a company builds its corporate brand over time, we should endeavor to build our personal brand as well. On a personal level, try thinking of yourself as an actual brand name. Your personal brand is not dissimilar from the major brands such as Microsoft, Coach, General Electric, Amazon, Disney, Coke, and BMW. You have to get out in the real world and market your uniqueness.

There are essentially four ways a company can become demonstrably different and create a better perception for its brand.

1.  Name

2.  Features/benefits

3.  Product or service

4.  Unique way you market

By properly identifying each of these communications keys, a company can build its brand on a solid foundation.

A great example of a company hitting its communications keys on all cylinders is the Cabbage Patch Kid. Here's a doll that didn't look, feel, or smell any differently from any other dolls. Yet, the doll was one of the hottest Christmas toys two years in a row. Woe to thee that could not put this doll under the Christmas tree!

What made the doll so desirable? Simple. The Cabbage Patch Kid hit all the communication keys right on target. First of all, it had a memorable name: Cabbage Patch Kid. Second, it had a unique feature: It came with adoption papers. Third, the product was "demonstrably different," in that each doll was prepackaged with its own name. And fourth and most important was the unique way the doll was marketed—you didn't just buy a Cabbage Patch Kid, you adopted it! This distinguished the Cabbage Patch Kid brand from other doll and toy brands.

*Each of us marches to the beat of a different drummer.*
**—ANONYMOUS**

## Personal Brand Building

Remember, you are in charge of your own brand. When you stop and think about it, in essence, you're really the vice president of marketing for Me, Inc. Personal brand building is a process that offers your uniqueness to the outside world and packages your attributes and characteristics in a way that allows you to be "demonstrably different." Personal branding allows you to stand out in the crowd. It's a way to separate yourself from the rest of the pack. Your personal brand is a concise calling card as to what you truly stand for and how others perceive your attributes, skills, and values. Your good name should stand for something—your integrity, the way you treat people. What you do for others beyond yourself will go a long way in making your personal mark. Brand building creates a pulpit for who you are and what makes you unique that creates value for others.

It's important that your personal brand be aligned with your true calling and purpose in life. It must be consistent with the talents and contributions that you have to offer to the world.

We all need to do some personal brand building. Ask yourself:

- What are the positive features or characteristics that make you unique?

- How are you demonstrably different?

- Are your differences perceived by others? (Remember, perception is often reality.)

## The Communication Key Advantage

Another good example of a company with strong communication keys is Apple Computer.

1.  Name: Apple iMac.

2.  Features/benefits: combines power and ease of use.

3.  Product: very personal computers.

4.  The way they market: no more beige boxes. Build computers with style and color as well as power and function. Appeal to the customer's intelligence and their appreciation for good design by combining form and function.

Personal computers were fast becoming a commodity with little difference between a myriad of beige boxes. PCs could be made by IBM, Dell, Compaq, or a number of other manufacturers with few identifying characteristics, save for the name on the box. But, from the beginning, Apple refused to license its operating system with the exception of a brief licensing experiment. Recognizing the high cost of losing control over its universally loved brand name, Apple ended its foray into licensing. From that point forward, Apple computers were made only by Apple, and ran on Apple's operating system that was renowned for its intuitive structure and user-friendly interface. At the same time, the company built computers that were "demonstrably" different from other desktop computers—first, by altering the shape and configuration of the beige computer "boxes," then, by adding color and more sophisticated design features that combined form and function. Apple simply didn't look or feel like other computers. Finally, Apple had an aggressive educational program, effectively capturing young computer users and building brand loyalty. Apple's carefully constructed communication keys helped build a brand that enjoys intense brand loyalty today.

## What Do You Stand For?

A key element of personal branding is the positive perception people have of what we truly stand for. For instance, Dr. Martin Luther King Jr. stood for racial equality. Walter Cronkite stands for journalistic integrity. Comedian Bob Hope will always stand for entertaining our homesick troops overseas. Earvin "Magic" Johnson is perceived as a winner both on the basketball court and for the good things he does for the urban community. Tony Robbins is admired by many as a great personal motivator.

Having a good personal brand creates value for all of those around you. Your good values, unique personality, skills/talents, and accomplishments go a long way in differentiating you from those who do not possess your unique traits and capabilities. One of my mentors, Bill Ball, never finished high school. But he shared with others his best individual trait—his personal integrity. He used to say, "Your word is your bond. It is your torchbearer. Do what you say you're going to do or fix it. Your talent by itself will not make you a success. But the combination of talent and integrity will always allow you to stand out from the crowd."

It's important to remember that building your personal brand is a process. It doesn't happen overnight. Your personal brand represents the consistent things you do day in and day out that allows others to perceive your true value and uniqueness. It's no secret that one of the areas in which many dot-com companies were deficit was their miscalculation of the time it takes to build a brand. They thought they could work twenty hours a day for three years and ride off into the sunset. But it takes time to have other people see the value in your corporate brand—or for that matter, in your personal brand. To build a strong personal brand you need to intensely focus on that which you do that offers value. You need to build a bond of trust with your customers. Trust, as you know, is not given automatically, it's earned the hard way—over time.

When we send a package by FedEx, we trust it will get to the right place at the right time. We know that even if a package should get lost or misplaced the company has an excellent tracking system that will allow us to sleep comfortably at night. Retailers like Nordstrom and Chico's have liberal "no-worry" return policies that make us feel good about our purchases from their stores. When we fly Southwest Airlines we know that we're not only getting low fares but also one of the industry's best safety records (no fatal crashes as of this writing).

## You've Got to Specialize

One of the ways you can personally brand yourself is through the art of specialization, or *narrowcasting*. This is your ability to hone in and narrow the scope of who you are and what you represent. Don't try to be all things to all people. I call this "avoiding the clock-radio syndrome." When you purchase a clock radio, you sure as heck know you're not getting the best clock and you most certainly know you are not getting the best-sounding radio either. Don't be a clock radio! Pick something you're great at and go for it with gusto.

In business, one of the biggest differences between Europe and the United States is that in the States we specialize far more than our European counterparts. One of Europe's top job titles is called "Managing Director." This title would not fly in the States because it denotes a generalist versus a specialist. In our country, if you have a problem with your heart you go see a heart specialist. If your company needs a turnaround, you see a corporate turnaround specialist. I myself am known as a brand rebuilding specialist.

In their splendid book *The Brand Called You*, Peter Montoya and Tim Vandehey point out the various benefits of specialization.

- Differentiation. You set yourself apart by doing a few things well—not by trying to be all things to all people (that is, the clock-radio syndrome).

- Presumed expertise. When you tell people you are a specialist in something, they naturally think you have specific skill sets in that area.

- Perceived value. Simply put, specialists can demand more money. It's sort of like a special on the menu. If you tell people the seafood pasta is your house specialty, people will not only order it—they'd be willing to pay more for your special entrée.

- Understandable benefit. Your personal brand becomes more memorable when it focuses around a few very clear benefits. People are more likely to see value in something that they readily comprehend.

- Focused on strengths. If you specialize in things that you enjoy and do best, you'll do better work and probably make more money doing it.

Authors Montoya and Vandehey tie a nice ribbon around personal branding: "There's only one you. No matter where you've come from or what you've done, you're unique. When you thread your personality, passions, and history into your brand, you're making yourself stand out from any other brand in the market—even if others have exactly the same skills and training as you."

## Revel in Your Uniqueness

Let's pause here for a moment and talk a bit more about uniqueness. In the market section in chapter two we talked about pinpointing our strengths. Again, strength is defined as a strong or valuable attribute. However, uniqueness allows us to stand out from the crowd. Uniqueness allows us to be demonstrably different in the way we display or flaunt our strengths. Britney Spears is a good singer but what makes her unique is her incomparable stage presence. Apple Computer is more than just a good company, it has a unique communication style and an Apple speak tone all its own. Apple clearly is a company that strives to make a difference.

Personal brand building is similar to building a corporate brand: You have to get out there and market your uniqueness. In fact, you should revel in your uniqueness. I learned this firsthand while traveling to Red China in the early 1980s. This was the real Red China of over twenty years ago. There were no Coke machines, no luxury hotels. This was the China of great mystery and adventure!

One of my boyhood dreams was to visit the Great Wall of China, one of the Seven Wonders of the World. But on the day I arrived at the Great Wall, it was extremely cold— ten degrees below zero. With high, gusty winds, it was strongly suggested by my Chinese hosts that I postpone my trek up the wall. Unfortunately for me, I was returning home bright and early the next morning. So despite my host's weather warnings, I decided to climb the wall in the blustery cold.

Climbing the wall was such a thrill, I hardly felt a chill. In fact, I was the only person to brave the elements that day. Or so I thought. The fact is, I wasn't alone. I was greeted at the top of the wall by an elderly Chinese man proudly sporting a worn-out ABC Sports cap, which he claimed he received during the Ping-Pong diplomacy era. He spoke to me in perfect King's English, asking, "Do you like your hair?" To which I quickly responded, "Not really. Why do you ask?" Noting my rather distinctive strawberry-blond hair color, he explained, "Let me tell you something. Being Chinese, I am the most common species on Earth. Twenty percent of the world's population is Chinese. There are well over a billion of us. You, however, are one of the most unique species on Earth! You see, only one out of every six hundred fifty thousand people on Earth has your hair color. You should revel in your uniqueness!" He skipped a few beats, and then countered, "Of course, I'm not just talking about your hair! Each of us is unique in our own way."

Every individual is unique. If we weren't unique there would be little reason for us to even exist at all. If we were all the same, our world would be a boring place to live. We'd all be mere clones. Our world would lack color. It would be like watching all of life's magnificence in black-and-white TV. Author John Powell sums it up nicely: "You have a unique message to deliver, a unique song to sing, a unique act of love to bestow. This message, this one, this act of love has been entrusted exclusively to the one and only you."

Powell tells the story about a wonderful, wise teacher who asked his wide-eyed young students to go out and find a small, unnoticed flower somewhere in town. He then asked his students to put the flower under a magnifying glass to study in detail the veins in the leaves and shades of color in the petals. He asked them to study the symmetry of the flower. He reminded his students that the flower might have gone unnoticed and unappreciated if they had not found and admired it. The teacher then made the connection between flowers and people. People are a lot like flowers. Each one is different, carefully crafted, and above all, uniquely endowed. But you have to spend time with them to know this. So many people in this world go unnoticed and unappreciated because no one has even taken the time with and admired their wonderful uniqueness. Our uniqueness allows us to live in a multidimensional world. It allows us to appreciate the complimentary capabilities and various talents of other people around us.

One day our marketing team was working on a new marketing plan to help turn around our consumer electronics company that had fallen from its former market leadership position. In talks, our new chief financial officer was lamenting the fact that our marketing group wasn't paying enough attention to the financial part of the marketing plan. I looked to him in bewilderment and said, "Well, now, if we as marketing people did everything right when it came to finances, there would be no need for you and your unique financial talent." Our CFO smiled that knowing smile of his and said, "Carry on. I'll be here when you need me."

We all have our unique talents to contribute to the world. Unlike other species, all human beings are different and extraordinary in some way, we have different personal traits, different backgrounds, memories, talents, and characteristics. That's why when we take those inkblot tests, some of us see the young maiden while others view the same inkblot as the old hag. That's why to some, the glass is half empty, while to others the same glass is half full.

*We are all special. We all have something unique to offer.*
*Your very life because of who you are has meaning.*
—BARBARA DEANGELES

## Respecting Your Uniqueness

If we want to be all we can be in life and move ourselves towards our true calling or purpose, it's important that we respect our uniqueness. There are several ways to do this. First, we must internalize that each of us is extraordinary in our own right. I once asked a business colleague what he feared most. He replied: "My biggest fear in life is to be ordinary versus extraordinary." Secondly, we need to clearly define our uniqueness. What do we do best that can add value to others? Finally, we need to accept, and therefore, respect our uniqueness. In doing so, we will have more respect for ourselves and our abilities.

One of Apple's ad campaigns saluted the uniqueness in all of us. Let me hit on some key phrases: "Here's to the crazy ones. The misfits. The rebels. The troublemakers. The round heads in the square holes" . . . The ad closes with . . . "because the people who are crazy enough to think they can change the world are the ones that do. Think Different." So be unique! Dare to be different. But in your difference—make a difference that you were here on this planet.

Even a small difference can count for a lot. One day an old man was walking along the beach in the early morning and noticed the tide had washed thousands of starfish up on the shore. Up ahead in the distance he spotted a boy who appeared to be gathering up the starfish one by one and tossing them back into the ocean. He approached the boy and asked him why he spent so much energy doing what seemed to be a waste of time. The boy replied, "If these starfish are left out here like this, they will bake in the sun, and by this afternoon they will all be dead." The old man gazed out as far as he could see and responded, "But, there must be hundreds of miles of beach and thousands of starfish. You can't possibly rescue all of them. What difference is throwing a few back going to make anyway?" The boy held up the starfish he had in his hand and replied, "It's sure going to make a lot of difference to this one!"

*When it's all over, it's not what you were . . . it's whether you made a difference.*
—BOB DOLE

## Make a Difference

I was part of the team that launched Planet Inc., a line of environmentally safe household cleaning products that also clean terrifically well. The product line is distributed not only in health food stores but also in major supermarkets like Gelson's, Vons, Ralphs, and Safeway.

The original founders of Planet, Stefan Jacob and Allen Stedman, developed a product cleaning formula that was hypoallergenic and safe for the environment and aquatic life. The product is never tested on animals. In a small way the company is making a big difference on this planet we call Earth. Other companies like Ben & Jerry's reach out to make a difference. Although Ben & Jerry's ostensibly sell ice cream, they also serve humanity by giving a percentage of their profits back to charity.

You don't need to be a corporate entity to make a difference in this world. People from all walks of life are making a big difference on a daily basis. We need to look no further than our heroic firefighters, police officers, educators, doctors, and health-care professionals. They all make a difference—each and every day.

It's particularly wonderful to note that you're never too young to recognize the importance of making a difference. By the age of thirteen, Craig Kielburger had done more to change the world than most of us ever will. While reading the newspaper he came across an article about a twelve-year-old boy who escaped from a Pakistani factory where he had been shackled in a carpet-weaving room and forced to work inhumane hours every day. The boy's parents had sold him into slavery when he was only four years old. He was paid the paltry sum of three cents per day.

Craig was appalled. How could children be treated this way in this day and age? Craig looked into the problem and discovered that few North American organizations had focused in this area. Accordingly, Craig and a group of his friends started faxing questions to groups throughout the world and the Free the Children organization was born.

Craig felt compelled to visit these countries and see what child slavery was like. His parents gave permission to their young son to spend seven weeks visiting India, Bangladesh, Thailand, Pakistan, and Nepal with a twenty-four-year-old Asian friend. Among other places, they visited an Indian fireworks factory where ten-year-old children were frequently injured, maimed, or killed due to a lack of safety precautions.

In the six years since Craig's first trip, his student-run organization has made great strides. They have helped alert the world's media to the problems and freed or rehabilitated literally hundreds of child slaves.

Craig's group was also instrumental in promoting the rug-mark marketing emblem for handwoven rugs certifying that the carpet was produced without using child labor.

Free the Children groups are operating in sixty schools in rural areas of India. They are also building or reconstructing thirty-two schools in South America, providing milking animals and sewing machines to destitute families so they no longer have to depend on their children's labor income to survive. Along the way, Craig has met with such world leaders as the Dalai Lama and Pope John Paul II.

Is there something you've always wanted to do to make a difference for others? Take the first step.

## EXECUTIVE SUMMARY

This chapter focuses on building a brand over time. Communication keys provide the ways in which a company can be demonstrably different or unique from the competition.

Just as a company builds its brand, we as individuals should endeavor to build our own personal brand as well. We have to get out in the real world and market our uniqueness. We need to package our personal attributes and characteristics that make us stand out from the rest of the crowd. To be a strong personal brand, we should strongly consider focusing on that which we do that offers value to others.

We talked in chapter two about pinpointing our strengths, but uniqueness goes beyond strength. Our uniqueness allows us to stand out by displaying our strengths in a way that is demonstrably different.

## EXERCISE 1: WHAT DOES YOUR LIFE STAND FOR?

A. List the ways in which you are "demonstrably different" or unique.

_____

_____

_____

B. Walter Cronkite's name stands for journalistic and broadcasting integrity. Martin Luther King Jr.'s name represents racial equality. What does your good name stand for?

_____

_____

_____

## EXERCISE 2: SPECIALIZATION/NARROWCASTING

What one thing are you truly great at? How can you channel this greatness to make a difference to others? You might want to refer back to the Capitalize On Your Strengths exercise on page 25.

_____

_____

_____

## EXERCISE 3: MAKING A DIFFERENCE

Name three times in your life that you made a positive difference in helping others.

_____

_____

_____

## EXERCISE 4: YOUR PERSONAL BRAND

Write one sentence that describes your personal brand. (For example, I am a person who inspires and encourages others to reach their full potential.)

_____

_____

_____

### TIME TO REFLECT

*How are you unique or demonstrably different?*

*Have you made a positive difference in helping others?*

CHAPTER 7

# EXPAND YOUR REACH

## Creating a Legacy

*The only thing you take with you when you're gone is what you leave behind.*
—JOHN ALLSTON

In marketing parlance, "reach" is the medium you use to transport or deliver your message to your target audience. As Canadian writer Marshall McLuhan said, "The medium is the message." In short, the medium you select to broadcast or get your message out to the outside world is just as important as the message itself.

Until the technological revolution of the mid- to late 1990s, most companies stuck to the tried-and-true traditional media mix that included TV, radio, newspapers, magazines, direct mail, and billboards. Today, the more traditional media competes with mediums brought on by technological advances that deliver corporate messages to smaller and more specific targets—cable television, internet advertising, advanced telemarketing, targeted direct marketing, e-mails, and chat rooms offer a plethora of choice in a now-cluttered media landscape. But when it comes to reach, the corporate purpose remains the same—effectively reach as many people within your target customer group as possible.

*We don't inherit the world from our parents; we borrow it from our children.*
—GANDHI

Earlier in the book we talked about how true success always involves reaching out to others beyond ourselves. We discussed Ralph Waldo Emerson's broader, more encompassing definition of success. We talked about creating more *meaning*, not just more money. On a personal level, reach is doing what you do best to reach out to make the world (or just one person) a better place because of it. It's about taking what you do well and creating a positive rippling effect that will help others—beyond yourself.

Just as businesses extend their reach and establish their legacy by giving back to the community, an important part of the Marketing Plan for Life involves reaching out and improving the lives of others. If you can extend the good things you do to have a positive effect on others, you are beginning to form your own legacy. Legacy is not a matter of chance—it's a matter of choice. It's about reaching out to touch the lives of others. It's not about desiring more for just yourself—it's about desiring the best for the entire world around you. Author Herman Melville explains, "We cannot live only for ourselves. A thousand fibers connect us with our fellow men; and among those fibers as sympathetic threads, our actions run as causes, and they come back to us as effects."

Our legacy is like a torch that we pass on to future generations. It is the ultimate reach. It gives our life meaning that lives on beyond our lifetime. Our legacy allows us to leave a trace, however small, that we were on this earth. In a sense, our legacy gives us a large or even small part of personal human history. Creating your legacy is a win-win situation. We commit to fulfill the needs of others and we in turn receive the feeling of fulfillment. We give value and we feel more valued. In his enlightening book *Philegatia: Living a Vision, Leaving a Legacy*, Glenn E. Young-Preston sums up legacy succinctly: "It's truly a case where the giver becomes the receiver and the receiver becomes the giver."

*The measure of a human being is not in their deeds, but in the legacy they leave.*
—SCOTT SHUKER

## Creating a Legacy in Business

Leaving a lasting legacy is something that all businesses and all individuals strive for. There are several ways companies can create a legacy in a business context.

- **Creating a sense of community.** One effective way companies reach their target audience and establish a corporate legacy is by creating a sense of community. This can be accomplished by creating loyalty or membership programs that reward customer loyalty with higher discounts, special gifts, expedited service, and other exclusive offers. Membership in these clubs clearly has its privileges. Frequent-flyer programs offered by the airlines are a great example of this. The more you fly, the more you fly free. The more you fly, the less you have to wait in line.

- **Event marketing.** A well-planned event can also allow a company to reach out and build community and loyalty among its target customers. Event marketing can be indirect by sponsoring an athletic contest, fashion show, chili cook-off, beauty contest, or any other event that is consistent with the brand's image and target audience. That's why you see so many beer companies reach for their twenty-one-to-thirty-five demographic by sponsoring marquee events for their age group including pro volleyball tours, concert tours, and loads of football games and NASCAR auto races.

- **Reaching out beyond target customers.** A good company's reach should extend beyond media and loyalty clubs. It's important that a company reaches out to the community at large by participating in social, charitable, and community causes. In an age of lightning-fast sound-bite-driven public opinion, it's more important than ever for companies to become good corporate citizens. Many top companies achieve their citizenry by giving back through charitable donations, setting up foundations, or creating their own community or charitable programs. These donations, foundations, or programs usually support causes near or dear to the company's leadership and corporate culture.

Media, event sponsorship, and club memberships fulfill a sense of community and promote brand loyalty for companies. Increasingly, companies are reaching out beyond the balance sheet. They are realizing that it is just as important to reach out to help make the world or community a better place to live. By developing "cause marketing" programs through endowments, foundations, and other socially responsible and charitable works, a company can reach out not only to their customers but to the world community. By improving and enhancing the lives of others, good companies are not only forming a responsible corporate culture but a legacy of their own.

## Forming Your Personal Legacy

Achieving our personal legacy can come in several different forms.

### Raising Children

We all get a lot of joy in watching our children grow up around us. We watch them as they develop in variations of our own character or likeness. When you stop and think on it, our kid's lives, accomplishments, and contributions to society are inexorably linked to our own legacy. We revel in the success of our children. When things don't go well, we feel their pain as if it were our own.

Remember, however, there's no written guarantee that your children will reflect your value system in a positive way. The apple doesn't always fall near the tree. Don't automatically expect that your children will necessarily follow in your footsteps or share your same value system. You need to make your own mark. Don't try to live your life vicariously through your kids. If you do, you could be setting yourself up for a short-lived legacy.

A family had a genuine antique vase in their home that had been handed down to them through several generations. It was a real treasure that was kept on the mantel as a special object of enjoyment. One day the parents returned home to be greeted at the door by their teenage daughter. "Mom and Dad," said the daughter, "you know that antique vase that you told us has been passed down from generation to generation?" "Yes," answered the parents. "Well, Mom and Dad, . . . our generation just dropped it."

It's my personal belief that sometimes we exert too much pressure on our kids or grandkids to carry on our legacy, traditions, or other vital interests, such as keeping our company thriving long after we're gone from this planet. Even if your immediate family carries your torch, it is probably unrealistic to think that succeeding generations will necessarily carry the same torch into their future. The nature of our life cycles dictate that each new generation is different and with these differences comes change. But one thing is resoundingly clear—a good legacy has the *potential* to be passed on to future generations to make the world a better place to live.

> *The only thing you take with you when you're gone is what you leave behind.*
> —JOHN ALLSTON

## Work

For many of us (especially those without children), work is often the most significant way to create a legacy. All of us—whether we're business executives, doctors, lawyers, designers, scientists, writers, truck drivers, or street sweepers—want our work to be recognized and appreciated. Good architects want to build things that are timeless and enduring. People in health, education, and social work have hope that their work as nurses, educators, and counselors will create a legacy of enriched lives for generations to follow. Look, let's face it: We all can't win a Super Bowl or win a Nobel Peace Prize, but our good work and deeds can certainly make a meaningful positive statement.

When it comes to meaningful work, I always think about my sister Karen. Karen is a nurse. But she has been referred to by many as an "angel of mercy." She often finds herself working with terminally ill patients. She helps her patients die with dignity. She, like other wonderful nurses, provide both physical and spiritual comfort to her patients. Comfort comes in many different forms. Sometimes she just listens to her patients; sometimes she's making a bed more comfortable, or a pillow fluffier, a room lighter or darker. Most of all, Karen says it's about "dying in peace and comfort." It's about letting terminally ill patients believe that something good will happen. The key to helping other people, she says, is "not being afraid to die yourself." My sister's legacy, like that of so many other nurses, will be that she provided dignity and comfort to those that needed it most.

Screenwriter Phil Alden Robinson, who wrote the screenplay for the movie *Field of Dreams*, made a wonderful personal statement when he was nominated for an Academy Award and lost. In a TV interview, a reporter asked him if he was disappointed that he didn't win the Oscar for best screenplay. Robinson replied that he had already won his Oscar. His award came from the hundreds of letters he received from sons telling him that he helped them reconnect with their fathers.

## Charitable Causes/Giving Back to the Community

The premium ice-cream maker Ben & Jerry's created the Ben & Jerry's Foundation. Its mission is to make the world a better place by working toward the elimination of the underlying causes of environmental and social problems. In addition to this ambitious mission, the company conducts socially aligned sourcing. The company believes it can drive social change through the power of everyday business decisions. This includes buying milk and cream from socially and environmentally responsible vendors. Ben & Jerry's also operates a Partner Shop program where Ben & Jerry's Scoop Shops are owned and operated by community-based nonprofit organizations. These ambitious examples of reaching out to the community are totally consistent with the 1960s-era activism culture practiced by the company's founders.

Our legacy may include donating not only money but time to causes that we truly believe have enduring value. These causes can include some of the following:

- Preserving the history and legacy of others

- Knocking down racial barriers

- Preserving our environment

- Helping make sick people laugh

- Contributing to our inner-city urban communities

- Serving as an ambassador for peace and freedom around the world

- Encouraging and enhancing the vitality of the arts

- Dedicating yourself to helping find a cure for a dreaded disease

- Providing a terminally ill child with a summer camp of joy

Steven Spielberg may just as likely be remembered for his preservation of the Holocaust survivors' legacy, via video, than for his Academy Award–winning films. In 1994, after filming the movie *Schindler's List*, Spielberg founded the Survivors of the Shoah Visual History Foundation. The foundation's mission is to videotape, collect, and preserve the testimonies of Holocaust survivors and witnesses. As of this writing, the Shoah Foundation has collected over fifty thousand eyewitness testimonies in fifty-seven countries and thirty-two languages. The foundation is totally committed to ensuring a worldwide, effective, educational use of its archive. While the foundation continues to conduct interviews, the focus has shifted to cataloging the testimonies and eventually making them accessible to the world. Spielberg took his talents and kicked it up a notch for a higher cause.

Jackie Robinson was a great overall athlete and Hall of Fame baseball player, but his real legacy is that he paved the way for others to follow. In 1947, when he came up to the major leagues with the Brooklyn Dodgers, it was a historic move that ended decades of discrimination against minorities in major professional sports. Robinson's legacy, however, clearly transcended baseball. He later became an outspoken leader in civil rights, a socially responsible corporate executive, a civil servant, and a major figure in national politics.

In 1973, a year after he died, his wife, Rachel, founded the Jackie Robinson Foundation. The foundation continues Jackie's fight for human dignity by supporting college-bound minorities and poor young people in developing their potential. The foundation carries out the courageous leadership that was the essence of Jackie Robinson's life.

Paul Newman's legacy has been much more than that of the superstar actor. His company, Newman's Own, offers among other products a line of salad dressings and spaghetti sauces. Every single cent of the company's after-tax earnings goes to charity. Newman has given more than $125 million to charitable causes ranging from the Hole in the Wall Gang Camp for terminally ill children to the Scott Newman Center for drug and alcohol abuse—named after his only son who died of an accidental overdose. Newman is also active in education and drought-relief programs in Africa.

Newman's Hole in the Wall Gang Camp, founded in 1988, is a nonprofit residential camp ingeniously designed as a Wild West hideout in northwestern Connecticut. More than a thousand children with cancer or other serious blood diseases come to Newman's camp each year, free of charge. The camp provides the children with camaraderie, fun, and a renewed sense of just being a kid.

Newman is quite vocal on the subject of philanthropy. "The concept that a person who has a lot should hold his hand out to someone who has less is still a human trait."

## Mentoring

Being a mentor is one of life's higher callings, especially for those who are approaching midlife or beyond. The great satisfaction in mentoring is that you can help develop others to become all they can be.

Mentors give, but they also get great satisfaction back from sharing their own knowledge and skills and watching others grow because of this sharing. Ralph Waldo Emerson said, "It is one of the most beautiful compensations of this life that no man can sincerely try to help another without helping himself." True mentoring is not about making your dreams happen—it's about making the dreams of others happen. Beware of trying to mentor those who don't want to be mentored! The result will be more like Professor Higgins in *My Fair Lady* than *Tuesdays with Morrie*. There are many people out there hungry for your wisdom and expertise—be receptive! Be there for them when they need you.

On a personal level, I've always had wonderful mentors. They allowed me to be all I could be and reined me in only when it became absolutely necessary (that's just before you make a complete fool of yourself). My mentor at Motorola, Ed Reavey, was the one who originally taught me the Twelve-Point Marketing Plan discipline—on the business side. My other mentor, Don Mainwaring, taught me how to apply the plan back to life in general. Both mentors gave me the original foundation for this book. When I asked what I could give them back in return, they both echoed the same thing: "Give back by being a good mentor to somebody else."

## Everyday Good Deeds

Little things mean a lot. A legacy can be born out of doing lots of good things for people everyday. They can be small things like making time to listen or being a friend in a time of need. It can be as simple as making someone laugh so they temporarily forget about their pain or illness. It could be the good values you share with others, or the occasional dollar you throw into a tin cup. It could be the call you make to your sick aunt. Legacy doesn't necessarily mean you have to achieve monumental history- or book-worthy accomplishments.

In the enduring Christmas classic *It's a Wonderful Life*, we come to recognize that George Bailey (played by Jimmy Stewart) truly had a wonderful life because of the little things he did everyday that touched and influenced other people's lives in a meaningful way. We're reminded through this wonderful Christmas classic that every man's life is important, especially when he makes a positive impact on the lives of others.

*A rock pile ceases to be a rock pile the moment a single man contemplates it, bearing within him the image of a cathedral.*
—ANTOINE DE SAINT-EXUPÉRY

## Searching for a Higher Meaning

Look at what you do and search for a higher meaning. A journalist was interviewing people and asking them about their jobs. The journalist came upon a bricklayer and asked him what he did all day. "Can't you see!" said the bricklayer. "I mix mud, water, and straw all day for fourteen hours a day. Sometimes when I get bored I mix water, mud, and straw just to relieve the repetition." Then the journalist moved on to the next worker who was apparently doing the exact same thing. "Excuse me, what is it that you do?" "Why, can't you see?" exclaimed the worker. "I'm building the foundation for the most beautiful cathedral on earth!"

They are both bricklayers—but one man has put his job into the context of a higher meaning. He was building cathedrals, not merely laying bricks.

*You are here to enrich the world, and you impoverish yourself if you forget the errand.*
—WOODROW WILSON

When Apple founder Steve Jobs was trying to recruit John Sculley, the president of Pepsico, he tried to appeal to Sculley's sense of a higher purpose and legacy. Sculley asked Jobs, "Why should I leave Pepsico?" Jobs stared straight at Sculley and said without skipping a beat, "Do you want to spend the rest of your life selling sugared water, or do you want to change the world?"

Personally, my prime motivation in writing this book was to give something back. If the same marketing-plan process I used to steer companies in the right direction could be reapplied to help others, maybe it will allow me to feel better about myself. Maybe in a small way, writing this book is part of my contribution—a small part of my legacy to help others who are on the same journey as me. Maybe part of my legacy will be to make meaning as well as money.

In his introduction to his best-selling book *What Should I Do with My Life?*, author Po Bronson adds his perspective on legacy: "We want to know where we're headed—not to spoil our own ending by ruining the surprise, but we want to ensure that when the ending comes, it won't be shallow. We will have done something. We will not have squandered our time here."

We pass on our personal torch to future generations by reaching out to others. Start now to make your contribution to the world around you. When you do, you have the potential to leave behind a legacy that will live long after you are gone.

## EXECUTIVE SUMMARY

Chapter seven deals with the various mediums that a company uses to reach its target audience. Beyond the media, good companies extend their reach by getting involved in the community, donating to charities, or setting up foundations to support special causes. Through these philanthropic endeavors, a company reaches out to both their customers and the community at large.

On the personal side of the ledger, we are reminded that true success always involves reaching out to people beyond ourselves. Reach is about doing what you do best to make the world a better place. The ultimate reach is legacy. Legacy is like a torch that we pass on to future generations. Our legacy reserves for us a small piece of personal human history. Legacy can be achieved in different forms: raising children, giving back to the community, our work, mentoring, and just plain everyday good deeds. Whatever we do in life, we should reach out to others to achieve a higher meaning or purpose.

## EXERCISE I: DEFINE YOUR LEGACY

A. If you died tomorrow, what would your legacy most likely be?

_____

_____

_____

B. Would you be satisfied with this legacy? Why or why not?

_____

_____

C. Write down the epitaph that you would like to see imprinted on your tombstone. Start with: Here lies a person who...

_____

_____

_____

_____

## EXERCISE 2: YOUR LEGACY—WHERE WILL IT COME FROM?

Your legacy can come in several forms. Choose the most likely form(s) in which you can best express your legacy. (Please explain.)

A.  Family/children

_____
_____
_____

B.  Meaningful work

_____
_____
_____

C.  Charitable causes

_____
_____
_____

D.  Giving back to the community

_____
_____
_____

E.  Mentoring or coaching others

_____
_____
_____

F. Keeping a positive attitude toward others

_____

_____

_____

G. Everyday good deeds

_____

_____

_____

H. Other—please explain

_____

_____

_____

## EXERCISE 3: MENTORING

A. Who was the most significant mentor in your life?

_____

B. What positive contribution did your mentor make toward the way you reach out to others?

_____

_____

_____

### TIME TO REFLECT

*If you died tomorrow, what would be your legacy?*
*Would you be satisfied with this legacy?*

# CHAPTER 8

# BUILD A HIGH-IMPACT ADVERTISING CAMPAIGN

## Reawakening the Creativity Within You

*All children are artists. The problem is to remain an artist once we grow up.*
—PABLO PICASSO

Agood ad campaign captures the true personality and lifestyle of the brand. It gets to the very heart and soul of what a company is all about and communicates this message in a compelling, creative way that reaches the target customer.

Just as a good advertising campaign captures the very heart and soul of a company, our innate creative talents allow us to share our own special DNA, vision, and creativity with the outside world. The key question is, How do we unleash this creativity? How do we overcome our internal barriers and reawaken the creativity that resides in all of us?

A great "ad" campaign requires these seven key elements:

1. Vision: The ability to see the end result by focusing on a clear, concise purpose.

2. Creative impact: Creating a message with impact that punches through loud and clear.

3. Presentation dynamics: It's not just what you present; it's the way you present it.

4. Reach: Spreading the word to the target audience in the most effective manner.

5. Frequency: Creating as many favorable impressions as many times as economically possible.

6. Buy in (take action): Make no mistake about it—the ultimate objective of any good advertising campaign is to get people to buy into your product or service. Advertising legend David Ogilvy used to say, "If it doesn't sell, it isn't creative."

7. Feedback: Advertising campaigns are increasingly tested and post-tested to make sure the campaign is delivering the intended message.

An effective ad campaign literally builds on the first seven points of the marketing-plan process, enabling the company to show a consistent presentation to the target customer. This footprint or look allows the company to build a lasting consumer impression over time.

The most important thing you need to know about the advertising and creativity section is that it's the eighth point of the marketing-plan process, not the first. Many companies want to start here. But you can't start a marketing plan with an advertising campaign. A great ad campaign is a natural outgrowth of the prior planning steps. Think of the marketing-plan process as a veritable symphony, with each part integral to the success of the whole.

In business or in life, there are no easy shortcuts. Before you can create personal impact, leave a lasting impression, and share your creative heart and soul with the outside world, you need to complete the first seven steps of your life plan. As a refresher course, let's review these important steps:

- Define who you are

- Capitalize on your strengths

- Discover the authentic you

- Find your personal niche

- Reinvent yourself

- Build your personal brand

- Create your legacy

Advertising icon William Bernbach sums up the importance of making a lasting impression in business or in life: "The truth isn't the truth unless people believe in you, and they won't believe in you if they don't know what you're saying, and they can't know what you are saying if they don't listen to you, and they won't listen to you if you're not interesting and you won't be interesting unless you say things imaginatively, originally and freshly." Later in this chapter we'll talk about how we as individuals can punch through loud and clear by presenting ourselves in a dynamic way—allowing our voice to be heard above the noise.

## Classic Ad Campaigns

Great ad campaigns require presentation dynamics and creative impact. But this doesn't necessarily mean that it has to be a great work of art. Some of the most memorable (and productive) classic advertising campaigns have been the simplest (and often annoying). Charmin bathroom tissue's "Please don't squeeze the Charmin" campaign was an ad that people loved to hate, but it also gave Charmin a distinct identity and point of difference in a product category that could be defined as a commodity—with little difference between brands—while making Mr. Whipple's distressed grocer character a household name. Alka-Seltzer's "I can't believe I ate the whole thing" brought a common ailment to the forefront, in a plain and simple language, and offered effective relief. And Eveready's Energizer Bunny was called by marketing experts "the ultimate product demo" because it does such an effective job of showcasing the product's unique selling proposition—long-lived batteries—in an inventive, fresh way. The Energizer Bunny has truly kept "going and going", appearing in more than 115 spots in English and Spanish.

More recently when the BMW Group's Mini Cooper was preparing for its stateside launch in 2001, the brand faced several obstacles. The model was virtually unknown in the United States, despite the company's assertion that its brand enjoyed icon status in the United Kingdom and Europe. In addition, the car's 2001 U.S. launch was seemingly ill timed—the U.S. auto market was dominated by SUVs, Japanese and German brands topped the import segment, and small car sales were at their fifteen-year low point. Finally, Mini's brand heritage was British, which was often linked to unreliability in the car category.

The advertising agency Crispin Porter + Bogusky set out to not only build the brand but also, in light of Mini's strong status on the other side of the Atlantic, to actually create an icon in the United States. Account planners found that the target customer was not a traditional demographic, but rather a psychographic defined by similar values and a way of thinking. Accordingly, they targeted the ad campaign toward those who "love to drive and wanted to choose their own path."

These objectives were accomplished by creating an alternative culture of driving called "motoring," where both product and customer resided. Mini's unique "motoring" sensation was communicated through unique product imagery, interactive print treatments including stickers, eye-catching billboards, and clever copy emphasizing the joy of driving that went beyond simply getting from point A to point B. The campaign was a smashing success. Crispin Porter + Bogusky reported that brand awareness reached 80 percent after one year of marketing, and sales surpassed projections each month since the launch.

Other ad slogans successfully delivered their message and had people singing along at the same time. Examples include Campbell Soup's "Mmm, mmm, good," Coke's "It's the real thing," Burger King's "Have it your way," and "I wish I were an Oscar Mayer weiner," by that very famous hot dog company.

These successful campaigns clearly reached their target customers, communicated their strategy in a creative and often fun way, and resulted—more often than not—in increased sales.

## Word of Mouth

Perhaps the most effective form of advertising is by word of mouth: one person telling another that something is good about your product or service (of course, it could also be bad). Word-of-mouth advertising creates a "whispering campaign" that can bode well or ill for your company. Today's chat rooms provide ample forum for this type of feedback. In today's world, whether you ask or not, you're going to get feedback. So you might just as well know what people are saying about your product or service.

In life as well as business you are in large part how you are perceived. Many personal reputations have been enhanced or tarnished by a positive or negative word-of-mouth whispering campaign. All in all, it's probably best to know what people are saying about you. Whether you act on this feedback largely depends on the respect or lack of respect you have for the person who is imparting the information.

## Share of Mind Versus Share of Market

A successful ad campaign not only creates increased share of market but increased share of mind. Share of mind allows a company to separate itself from the pack. It creates a deeper relationship with the target audience because the heart, guts, and soul of the brand is revealed to the customer. For instance, Apple Computer has share of mind, IBM does not. It is literally imbedded within you at a very early age that creative people should prefer Macs over PCs. In fact, in most creative corporate environments, Mac owners would rather "fight than switch." Other examples: Volkswagen's Beetle has share of mind, Hyundai does not. In the world of motorcycles, Harley-Davidson has great share of mind and a genuine personality. I dare say that Honda does not.

Even as individuals we should always strive for top-of-mind awareness versus back-of-mind awareness. One of the ways you achieve top-of-mind awareness is by being who you really are and reveling in your uniqueness as discussed in earlier chapters. A public-relations colleague of mine often muses, "It's better to be known for something than to be known for nothing."

*The intuitive mind is a sacred gift and the rational mind is a faithful servant. We have created a society that honors the servant and has forgotten the gift.*
—ALBERT EINSTEIN

## Left Brain/Right Brain

On the personal side of the ledger, in discussing creativity it makes sense to delve a bit deeper into the two types of individual mind-sets or different ways of thinking. Logical or left-brain people tend to view things differently than creative or right-brain people. The left-brain/right-brain concept was developed from the research done by psychobiologist Roger W. Sperry, who discovered that human beings have two very distinct ways of thinking. The following table illustrates some of the key differences of our left-brain/right-brain ways of thinking.

| LEFT BRAIN | RIGHT BRAIN |
|---|---|
| Uses logic | Uses feeling |
| Detail oriented (looks at parts) | Big-picture oriented (looks at whole) |
| Objective | Subjective |
| Uses numbers and facts | Uses imagination |
| Reality centered | Fantasy centered |
| Conservative | Risk taker |
| Pragmatic | Intuitive |
| Rational | Creative |
| Thinks step-by-step | Thinks outside the box |
| Connects the dots | Connects the seemingly unconnected |

Although you often hear people say I'm a left-brain person or a right-brain person, it's important to note that creativity (the right brain) resides in all of us. In fact, we're born with a significant amount of right-brain expression. Just observe a child's total sense of wonderment. Watch how they play make-believe games or how they tinker with their toys. Marvel at their finger-painting creativity that always seems to find a special place on our refrigerator door. Think about a child's wonderful ability to transport themselves to a world of fantasy.

## Creativity Diminishes as We Get Older

Unfortunately, research shows that we lose a lot of our childlike creativity as we get older. In fact, our propensity to generate original ideas reduces from 90 percent at age five to 20 percent at age seven. Regrettably, by the time we reach adulthood, creativity remains in only 2 percent of our entire adult population. One of the reasons our creativity seems to be diminishing is that in today's society we tend to use our left brain more than our right. Today's educational system seems to focus on mathematics, language, and logic. Our left brain also comes heavily into play as we deal with the everyday chores of life, including balancing the checkbook, handling our administrative duties, or just going through all the political red tape at work.

## Creativity and Perfection

It's not that we totally lose our creative skills; it's just that we need to rekindle the creative spirit that lies within us. So here's the key question: How do we reawaken the creativity that resides in all of us? Julia Cameron, in her classic book *The Artist's Way*, suggests that when it comes to creativity we should not try to be too much of a perfectionist. Most of us fear that we won't write the perfect book, the perfect screenplay, make the perfect presentation, throw a perfect party with perfect guests, hit that perfect note, or perform that perfect audition. Let's face it: There will always be room for improvement in any creative endeavor. Very few of us nail a masterpiece on our first try. The world of creativity is chock-full of revisions, rewrites, and if-at-first-you-don't-succeed type scenarios. But at some point you have to fish or cut bait. Any film editor will tell you that a movie is never quite cut perfectly. Any author will tell you a book is never really completed. An artist will tell you that their painting was never really finished—they just ran out of canvas. But at some point even creative people have to meet the reality of deadlines or they'll never be able to share their creativity with the outside world.

Consider the quintessential Renaissance man, Leonardo da Vinci. He was an all-purpose creative talent as a sculptor, painter, engineer, architect, and inventor. He was not just a jack-of-all-trades—he actually mastered all of them. But Leonardo had a big flaw—he had a hard time finishing his projects. He had so many projects going on at once, he had difficulty completing any single endeavor. His lack of focus prevented him from ever achieving financial independence. His failure to discipline his creative talents also deprived the world of a lot of his true greatness. Remember: Your art and creativity are only a gift when you actually finish what you start.

When it comes to creativity, perhaps Julia Cameron asks the core question: "What would I do if I didn't have to do it perfectly?" Do you have an answer?

*If you have a voice within you that says, "you cannot paint," then by all means paint, and that voice will be silenced.*
**—VINCENT VAN GOGH**

## Reawaken Your Creative Spirit

So where am I taking you here? Simple. Don't put your creativity on hold! Don't live life vicariously in the creative dreams of others. Stop telling yourself it's too late. Unlock your own creativity—now. Let the creativity that resides deep within your veins flow freely. Regardless of how you do it, it's important to reawaken the creativity that lies dormant within you. For instance, if you always wanted to learn how to play the guitar, take lessons now. If you always wanted to paint, buy some paint, brushes, and an easel and start painting. If you always wanted to be a mentor, find somebody who needs mentoring. If you always wanted to be a dynamic speaker, get in front of an audience. If you always wanted to be a gourmet cook, take some cooking lessons or invite a few guests over to try your new recipe for eggplant parmesan. If you always wanted to climb mountains, start climbing. If you always wanted to write a book or screenplay, start pounding those keyboards. All of us have our own form of creativity. Don't let it lie dormant—take action and express your own art form as a gift to the outside world. Famous producer Frank Capra once said, "A hunch is creativity trying to tell you something." All of us have our own form of creativity.

## Presentation Dynamics

When it comes to expressing your creativity, sometimes it's not just what you present, it's the impact you make when you present it. I call this the art of "Presentation Dynamics."

As a young marketing executive with Motorola, the art of presentation dynamics played a pivotal role in securing the approval of my target audience. Let me set the scene for you. Part of my job was to present our annual TV advertising campaign to our top five hundred retail accounts. When it came to advertising, this group was hard to impress. They all envisioned themselves as self-appointed advertising experts. Every year I'd have the same problem in presenting our TV ad campaign to this group. Half the group loved the campaign—the other half hated it. We could never seem to get their total approval.

After several years of frustration, I put my own creative plan of presentation dynamics into action at our annual meeting. I addressed the retailer group by admitting that because we were all advertising experts, it made it tough to please everybody. I gained their empathy by telling them that it was nearly impossible to gain unanimous approval for something as subjective as advertising. I told them how I really felt by singing them a song that I co-wrote entitled "Everyone's an Advertising Expert." It was a long time ago but the song went something like this:

> "Everyone's an advertising expert. Everyone knows how it should be done and just when you get the thumbs up on what everybody thinks, the window washer peers in and says, you know, that ad really stinks!"

I know what you're thinking, "don't quit my day job." But, you know my little song worked! After gaining my audience's understanding (not to mention empathy) they gave my new ad campaign their unanimous approval. For the first time in my young career I got to exit stage left with a thumbs up and a thundering round of applause. Again, sometimes it's not only what you present—it's the impact you make presenting it.

> *There's one thing stronger than all the armies in the world,*
> *and that is an idea whose time has come.*
> —VICTOR HUGO

## The Creative Process

When it comes to harnessing creative ideas there is no right way or wrong way. But one thing is clear: Creativity is indeed a process. In his now-classic book *A Technique for Producing Ideas,* James Webb Young teaches us to think within a creative process to generate ideas. His outline is delightfully simple, but it works:

1. Gather your information

2. Digest your information and blend it into your mind

3. Sleep on the information

4. Give birth to the idea

5. Put the idea into action in the real world

The very soul of creativity lies with the generation of a relevant and exciting idea. This holds true whether you're a business executive, teaching professional, computer programmer, advertising copywriter, or even a do-it-yourself home designer. But facing a dark computer screen or blank sheet of paper can be an intimidating and daunting experience. Even if you think you've never had a creative idea in your life, I suggest you try Young's simple but highly effective process. It will help you smash through any mental barriers that might prevent you from unleashing your creativity on the outside world.

## Creative Rituals

When it comes to stimulating our creative energy, everybody seems to have their way of doing things. Each of us has rituals that can kick start our creative intensity. Here are some rituals that people tell me they have used to put themselves back into a creative flow and mood.

- Take a shower
- Listen to classical music
- Go jogging
- Take a brisk walk
- Work out
- Take a short nap
- Read passages from a great writer
- Meditate
- Use affirmations
- Work in the garden
- Read the newspaper
- Have stimulating conversations with people you admire
- Take a break
- Walk on the beach
- Carry a notepad to jot down your thoughts
- Carry a small tape recorder
- Make love

- Go shopping
- Continue to write
- Get right back at it!

*Discovery consists of seeing what everybody has seen and*
*thinking what nobody has thought.*
—ALBERT VON SZENT-GYÖRGYI

## The Creative Environment

Your environment can have a major influence on your ability to be innovative and creative. The environment around you sets the stage or mood for you to be at your innovative best. The right environment can provide the stimuli you need to get your creative juices flowing.

The 3M Company goes to great lengths to provide a corporate environment that allows its employees to "think outside the box." The company encourages its researchers to spend 15 percent of their time on subjects that interest them. This creative corporate value system has often paid off handsomely for 3M. Perhaps the best example of this is Art Fry. Utilizing his 15 percent innovative free time; Fry came up with the idea of designing an adhesive paper that led to the marketing of Post-it Notes! Fry's idea hit the jackpot and has become one of 3M's most profitable office products. 3M doesn't muzzle ideas—they provide an environment that brings innovation and creativity out into the open.

*The world of reality has its limits; the world of imagination is boundless.*
—JEAN-JACQUES ROUSSEAU

It's extremely important to provide an environment that allows people to flaunt their innovative skills and creativity without setting up boundaries. I used to have a boss that set the stage beautifully for his advertising department by saying, "In my department sins of aggression will be more than tolerated, sins of omission will not." I've learned even in our corporate brainstorming sessions that setting the proper tone is vitally important for the creative process to flourish. In our creative sessions there are literally no bad or crazy ideas. Every idea is perceived as a great one. We eventually narrowcast the ideas, rework them, and extend the "best of the best" ideas to real-world applications. We then hitchhike off each other to make the idea even better. By the time we're done with the process we can't even remember where the great ideas came from—we just know we're ready to put them into motion.

Providing the proper environment has a lot to do with your own personal workspace. Look at the room in your house or office. Do your surroundings stimulate the creativity inside of you? Does your creative workspace get your juices flowing? Does the lighting in your workspace allow you to see things clearly? What about the noise level? Is it conducive to the level or concentration that you need? Do you have enough privacy? Is there artwork, decorations, or colors that will allow the real you to emerge? Do you have a comfortable chair to sit on or a comfortable table to work on? Many creativity experts agree that all these things are important to maximize the creative process.

But let me pass along this one personal insight. If you have passion and a purpose for your work, you can work just about anywhere. Some of the best writers and artists are so stimulated by their work that they can literally block out the world around them. I used to be extremely sound sensitive, but I find when I'm stimulated and I'm in alignment with my true purpose, I don't necessarily need the perfect place to light my creative fire. I no longer need crashing ocean waves or mountain greenery to get in gear. I can now work on a jam-packed plane, a noisy hotel room, or even in a crowded Starbucks. The more places you can work, the more productive you can become.

*Good art is not what it looks like, but what it does to us.*
—ROY AZDAK

## Handling Criticism

If there's one thing that can stop creativity right in its tracks, it's unjust feedback or criticism of our creative efforts. I'm not talking about constructive criticism that allows us to refine our work. I'm talking about nasty, personal, inaccurate, unwarranted, mean reviews, rendered by critics, pundits, and naysayers. Experts say the best thing to do when this happens is to strengthen your resolve, jump back on the horse, and resume your creative work. Renowned artist Paul Gauguin was heavily chastised for what his Paris critics called the "sensationalism" of his art. They thought much of his work was surreal and overstated. Yet, it was Gauguin who knew the truth. It was Gauguin who painted the beautiful reality of the pink-hued sandy beaches of Tahiti at sunset when the lighting was surreal and nearly perfect. Because his critics had never traveled to Tahiti, they were unaware of the reality of his native island work. It was only after Gauguin's death that he became one of the most famous and lauded artists of all time.

But sometimes, constructive criticism is absolutely vital for a company to provide an environment where people can flourish—both in our personal lives and in the workplace. One of my biggest concerns working with my corporate creative teams is that they sometimes lose sight of the marketing strategy by trying to be too artsy or too cute. It's important to be creative, but you can't lose sight of the fact you're trying to sell stuff. This is where solid constructive criticism comes into play.

> *Vision is the art of seeing the invisible.*
> —JONATHAN SWIFT

## Vision and Creativity

Vision is perhaps the best expression and manifestation of our creativity. Our vision provides a direction and purpose to create an attractive and attainable snapshot of the future. Our vision can inspire a single work of art or encourage an entire group of people to reach new heights. Are you a person of vision? Can you see the forest through the trees? Can you visualize the end result long before it actually happens? Visionary people often use "creative visualization." They visualize the end result long before it happens. We'll talk more about this mental rehearsal process in chapter ten.

Most of the world's greatest creators, inventors, and artists are true visionaries. Mozart was so attuned to his vision that some say he could actually see and hear the music in his heart, mind, and soul before he wrote it down.

Michelangelo was known to have said that he could see his completed work of sculpture in a huge block of marble—long before he began chiseling away at it. All he really needed to do was chisel out his vision.

When Dr. Jonas Salk was trying to discover the cure for polio, he knew the answers before he actually started research. Because he had a vision of where he was going, he had the ability to see through the details toward the end result.

On the business front, Amazon's visionary founder Jeff Bezos was told that nobody would ever buy quality books from a computer—especially when you can buy books at any bookstore. But Jeff saw the need for convenience and the ability to read book reviews on-line prior to purchase. His marketing vision is a great case study for any MBA student.

*Creativity might be as much found in a first-rate chicken soup*
*as it is in a third-rate painting.*
—ABRAHAM MASLOW

## Creative Impact

Because we ourselves are all creations, being creative comes with the territory of being a human being. Even if we don't receive the accolades or the label, we are all creative people. We all have the innate ability to leave an indelible mark or unique footprint in the sand of time. All of us have the need to create.

Perhaps the most satisfying part of creativity is the positive impact it can have on others. It could be as simple as creating a sensational deep-dish apple pie or making up an entertaining fairy tale to help put your kids to sleep. It could be a great book, a brilliant screenplay, or just creatively rearranging your living room furniture to create more space. It can be a magnificent painting or finding a shortcut on the way home. The point is, unleash and reawaken the creativity within you. Don't be afraid to go through the creative process. Struggle. Harmonize. Bemoan. Gather information. Meditate. Incubate. Redo. Reshape. Share jubilation. It's all part of the creative process.

We all have a masterpiece inside us just waiting to come out. So what are you waiting for?

## EXECUTIVE SUMMARY

The chapter reinforces the point that great advertising comes from a well-conceived total marketing plan. A great ad campaign is a natural outgrowth of the prior seven steps of the planning process. You need to complete points one through seven before you are truly ready to present your company's creative message to the outside world.

Similar to a great ad campaign that captures the very heart and soul of a company, our innate creative talents allow us to share our own special DNA, vision, and creativity to the outside world. We are all born with right-brain creativity, but research shows that we lose a lot of our childlike creativity as we grow into adulthood. It's not that we lose our creative skills; it's just that we need to reawaken the creativity that resides in all of us. We should not let fear of failure or lack of perfection put our creativity on hold. If you've always wanted to paint, start painting now. If you always wanted to write a book or screenplay, start pounding those keyboards. Find a creative environment that suits you. Don't overreact to unjust criticism. Harness your creativity and share your vision with the world around you.

## EXERCISE 1: UNLOCKING YOUR CREATIVITY

A. The left-brain way of thinking uses logic and is detail oriented, while the right brain uses feeling and is big-picture oriented. Would you describe yourself as predominately a left-brain or right-brain person? What are your major left- or right-brain characteristics?

| LEFT BRAIN | RIGHT BRAIN |
|---|---|
| 1. _____ | 1. _____ |
| 2. _____ | 2. _____ |
| 3. _____ | 3. _____ |
| 4. _____ | 4. _____ |
| 5. _____ | 5. _____ |
| 6. _____ | 6. _____ |

B. What were the most creative things you did as a child growing up?

_____

_____

_____

C. List the most creative things you have done as an adult.

_____

_____

_____

_____

D.  List three creative things you always wanted to do, but always postponed doing (for example, playing the guitar, taking a cooking class, learning to paint, etc.).

1. _____

2. _____

3. _____

E.  What creative things would you do if you weren't afraid of failure, concerned about criticism, or had the need to do things "perfectly" before you do them?

_____

_____

_____

_____

F.  What are the major stumbling blocks that prevent you from expressing your creativity?

_____

_____

_____

G.  List three action steps that you can take now to reawaken your creativity (for example, take a gourmet cooking class, guitar lessons, sing in you church choir).

1. _____

2. _____

3. _____

H.  Creative heroes: List three people whose creativity and life you admire most.

1. _____

2. _____

3. _____

I.   Setting creative goals: List the action steps that you will take over the next year to rekindle your creativity. As we'll discuss in chapter ten, your goals should be quantifiable; they should have time and numbers attached to them (for example, I'd like to finish my first book of poems during the next six months and have them published a year later).

_____

_____

_____

## EXERCISE 2: VISION

Are you a person who can see the forest through the trees? Can you visualize the end result before it happens? List two cases in your life when you exhibited vision.

1. _____

2. _____

### TIME TO REFLECT

*Have you put your creativity on hold?*
*Do you have a masterpiece within you just*
*crying to get out?*

# PLAN YOUR DISTRIBUTION

## Sharing Your Time and Energy Wisely

*Things that matter most should not be at the mercy of things that matter least.*
—JOHANN WOLFGANG VON GOETHE

In business, distribution is about deciding where to sell your product or service while remaining consistent with the business you're in. When planning your distribution strategy it's important not to stray off course. It's about being selective in choosing where to sell your product or service. If you want to maintain a high-end positioning for your product, you should probably think twice about selling at a discounter like Wal-Mart. Likewise, you're not likely to see Tiffany selling in the jewelry section of a mass-marketing retailer like Sam's Club. The fact is, when it comes to distributing your product and service, like it or not, you're often judged by the company you keep.

On a personal level, distribution is all about quality time management. It's about spending quality time with quality people. It's not going through the motions; it's about investing your time on those things that matter most to you. It's about taking timely action. It's not spreading yourself so thin that you can't deliver on the promises you made to yourself and other important people in your life. It's about spending your time wisely pursuing your true purpose or true calling in life.

## The Power of Positive Energy

On the personal side, distribution is also about spending your time with people who support you. As a child growing up, actress Jodie Foster was surrounded by positive feedback from her family and friends. Upon accepting the Academy Award for best actress, Foster held up her Oscar statuette and proudly proclaimed, "This is for my mother, who told me as a child that my finger paintings on the refrigerator were really Picassos."

No matter how much money we have or how much fame we've achieved, we all need to be around people who give us positive energy. Frank Sinatra was seventy-eight years old and still selling out all his concerts. On this particular night, in front of a packed audience, Sinatra couldn't remember the words to one of his standard songs—"All or Nothing at All." Try as he might, the words would not come to the aging superstar. Now, in his younger days brimming with confidence, Sinatra would easily brush this off with a self-deprecating joke and move on to another song. But at seventy-eight, and in the twilight of his career, Sinatra on this night seemed totally embarrassed. Embarrassed to the point that he told the packed house, "I'm very sorry . . . maybe I shouldn't be doing this anymore." As the star was about to shuffle off the stage for probably the last time, a voice in the highest section of the balcony rang out, "That's OK, Frank, we love you anyway." Then another voice echoed, "We love you, Frank." And then another voice rang out, "Come on back, Frank, we love you." Then almost in magical unison the entire audience gave him an enormous standing ovation. The teary-eyed star, obviously emotionally moved, came back on stage and sang the song he couldn't remember with the verve, poise, and passion of a fabulous talent in his prime. The positive energy Ol' Blue Eyes received from his audience pulled him through on a night when he really needed encouragement to stay focused on the moment.

. Spending quality time with quality people who mentor, motivate, and encourage you has always been an important element in achieving true success in life. Unfortunately, the reality of life doesn't always allow us to associate with positive-thinking people all of the time. However, we can certainly make a concerted effort to identify those people who give us the most positive energy in pursuing our goals, dreams, and aspirations. A high-achieving professional friend of mine has a simple but effective way of achieving this. He writes down those people who make his PE (positive energy) list. Those who send off negative energy make his NE list. His goal? Spend as much quality time as possible with the people on his PE list. He personally used this PE system to help make a remarkable recovery from life-threatening cancer. He surrounded himself with positive-energy people who encouraged and motivated him to beat the disease. He won his bout with cancer in part because of the support system around him.

Good companies always strive to provide an environment that supports and encourages its employees to reach their full potential. Women's apparel maker Chico's goes to great lengths to foster an environment of creativity for its employees. The company holds "Art at Work" exhibits that display the individual employee's works of art, ranging from landscape paintings, to custom-made jewelry, to handmade pottery. Even the employees' kids get in the act by displaying their delightful finger paintings (many of which were probably taken from the family refrigerator). Blue ribbons are awarded to winners by category. The company through events like these has found a lot of creative talent that might otherwise be buried in the accounting department.

Chico's not only encourages creativity, it also understands the value of employees "feeling in on things" and having a sense of connectedness as to what's going on in the company. In this spirit, Chico's chief financial officer hosts Friday beer parties at the end of the workday. Here, company colleagues are afforded the opportunity to mix and mingle and get to know what's happening in various departments throughout the firm. By offering a supportive environment that's also fun, Chico's employees seem to want to work harder to meet the company's goals.

## Be Where the Business Is

Another element of distribution is that you want your products or services to be sold in locations where the majority of business is most likely to occur. You want to put your company in the best position to maximize its sales. In short, you want to be where the action is. I personally had the misfortune to explain to our board of directors of a well-known boat company that our sales were excellent—except in places where there were large bodies of saltwater. That was highly unfortunate since we were in the business of selling boats. I subsequently explained that the hulls of our boats were not conducive to saltwater, therefore limiting our sales to freshwater lakes and reservoirs. The fix was simple: modify our hulls and increase sales by being able to sell our boats to both saltwater and freshwater regions. In short, position yourself to be where the business is.

Just as a company needs to position itself to maximize its sales, we as individuals need to put ourselves in the best position to succeed in life. It's been said, "If you want to be a blooming rose, don't plant yourself in the desert." We, like companies, need to get close to the action. For instance, if you aspire to be a great actor, perhaps you should consider moving to New York or Los Angeles and see how you stack up against the competition. If you want to be a country singer, you might consider moving to Nashville to get closer to the heart of the country-music business. Distribute yourself wisely—put yourself in position to score and hit your goals.

## A Question of Timing

When it comes to distribution, proper timing is everything. In a legendary ad campaign for Paul Masson wine, actor Orson Welles holds up his wine glass proudly and proclaims: "We'll sell no wine before its time." As mentioned earlier, Budweiser beer commercials flaunt the fact that its beer is fresher than its competition, reminding us to check the "born-on" date on the side of the can or bottle as a symbol of freshness.

Without a clear understanding of time and how to invest our time wisely, we'll have difficulty in achieving our goals, dreams, and aspirations. For starters, as A. Roger Merrill and Rebecca R. Merrill discuss in their illuminating book *Life Matters,* two types of time exist. There's *chronos* time—a Greek word meaning chronological time. *Chronos* time is linear; no minute is worth any more than any other minute. Time just marches on. The clock dictates the rhythm and beat of life. A key question in *chronos* time would be how many hours did you work today?

Then there's another type of time paradigm called *kairos* time—another Greek word that means appropriate or quality time. Here time is something to be experienced. It's not how much time you spend; it's what you do with your time that really matters. The essence of *kairos* time is in the value of the time, not in the numbers or hours spent. So the key question in *kairos* time would be not so much how many hours you worked, but what quality things did you accomplish with your time? Did you invest your time on those things that mattered most?

## Spending Your Time Wisely

In her famous Villanova commencement address, Pulitzer Prize–winner Anna Quindlen recounted the words of Senator Paul Tsongas spoke when he decided not to run for re-election because he was diagnosed with cancer: "No man ever said on his deathbed I wish I had spent more time in the office." Pastor Rick Warren, in his book *The Purpose-Driven Life,* reinforces Quindlen's sentiments:

> I have been at the bedside of many people in their final moments when they stand on the edge of eternity and I have never heard anyone say, "Bring me my diplomas, I want to look at them one more time. Show me my rewards, my medals, that gold watch that I was given." When life is ending, people don't surround themselves with objects. What we want around us are people—people we love and have relationships with. In our final moments, we all realize that relationships are what life is all about. Wisdom is learning that truth sooner than later. Don't wait until you're on your deathbed to figure out that nothing matters more.

Listen up for a minute. Even as I write this book, I know I'm on the same journey as you. I am finally beginning to recognize that the key to time is not just to spend it but to make a wise investment in it. Unfortunately, we often have this big gap between what is really important and how we actually spend our time. Here's the wake-up call: You'll never find time for anything important unless you make a commitment to make the time.

*Don't say you don't have enough time. You have exactly the same minutes and hours per day that were given to Helen Keller, Pasteur, Michelangelo, Mother Teresa, Leonardo da Vinci, Thomas Jefferson, and Albert Einstein.*
—H. JACKSON BROWN

By now you're recognizing there's a big difference between mere linear time management and quality time management—between spending time and *investing* time. Dr. Dan Baker points out in his book *What Happy People Know,* that each of us has exactly the same amount of time as the richest and most powerful people in the world. Even the wisest person has only twenty-four hours in a day. It's what we do with that day that counts. Baker concludes that "time is not a tyrant. Time is the great equalizer."

Life offers us the precious gift of time. But time also is fleeting and mysterious. None of us really know how much time we actually have left. That's why the gift of time is the most valuable gift you can give another person. Pastor Rick Warren explains: "Time is your most precious gift because you have only a set amount of it. You can make more money but you can't make more time. The most desired gift of love is not diamonds or roses or chocolates. It is focused on attention."

*If you want to make good use of your time, you've got to know what's important and then give it all you've got!*
—LEE IACOCCA

## Investing Time on That Which Matters Most

I was spending a delightful evening at a trendy restaurant in New York with a business associate of mine. Let's call him Don. He was an executive with a large apparel company. After several glasses of wine, Don started to lament that his personal life was almost in a shambles. He knew he wasn't spending enough quality time with his wife and two young kids. He also mentioned that he had a passion for golf and that he wished he had more time to improve his golf game. In short, he wanted to spend more quality time on the important things in his life, but he just couldn't seem to find the time—because he was so busy working. Listening intently, I asked him to draw two pie charts on the napkin in front of him. (Come to think of it . . . how trendy could this restaurant be if they were using paper napkins?)

On one pie chart I urged him to jot down how he would like to invest his time. As I looked at Don's pie chart, naturally a big percent of his pie was spending more quality time with his family; another slice of pie had to do with improving his golf game. Still another had to do with maintaining health, and yet another related to spending more quality leisure time. What was interesting was that his present job was just a mere average slice of the pie. The kicker came when I asked him to write another pie chart that revealed how he was actually spending his time.

# How Don would like to spend his time.

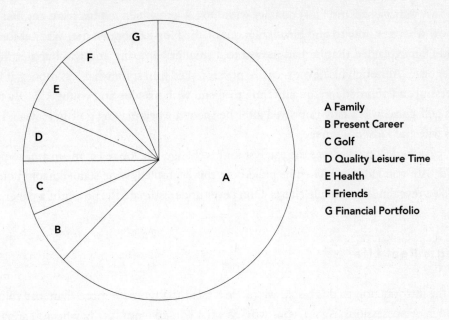

A Family
B Present Career
C Golf
D Quality Leisure Time
E Health
F Friends
G Financial Portfolio

# How Don is actually spending his time.

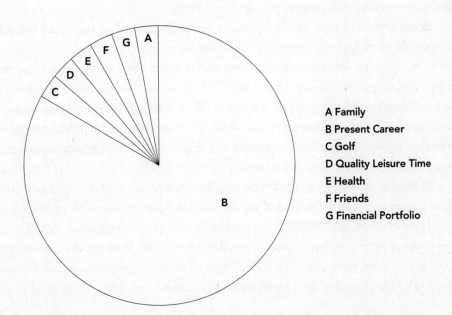

A Family
B Present Career
C Golf
D Quality Leisure Time
E Health
F Friends
G Financial Portfolio

You guessed it! His present job occupied the vast majority of his total pie with virtually no time left to focus on what mattered most to him.

A year passed and I lost contact with Don. I knew he'd left his company, but I didn't know where or how to find him. Then out of the blue he phoned me. We met for dinner, and Don explained that he had moved to a smaller company and was happier than he'd ever been. Although his new executive position paid him somewhat less money, it was less stressful and afforded him quality time to spend with his wife and young kids. By the way, his golf game was vastly improved after he spent a week playing golf in Hawaii. He took his wife and kids, of course.

I asked Don what was the catalyst for his change. He looked at me in amazement and said, "Are you kidding?" Then he pulled out this crumpled, wine-stained napkin out of his wallet, revealing the two pie charts. Don't ever underestimate the power of a paper napkin!

## Getting a Real Life

In the introduction to this book, we made it clear that you are more than just your work, career, or possessions. Again, your work is what you do—not totally who you are. Besides, you'll also be better at your work if you create a fuller, more purposeful life—a life of meaning, a life that goes beyond being just an executive, a lawyer, nurse, a teacher, a student, police officer, or whatever you do for a living.

Anna Quindlen again puts it in proper perspective for all of us: "Get a life, a real life, not a manic pursuit of the next promotion, the bigger paycheck, the larger house. Do you think you'd care so very much about these things if you blew an aneurysm one afternoon or found a lump in your breast? Get a life in which you notice the smell of saltwater pushing itself on a breeze over seaside heights. A life in which you stop and watch a red-tailed hawk circle over the water gap or the way a baby scowls with concentration when she tries to pick up a Cheerio with her thumb and first finger. Get a life in which you are not alone. Find people you love and who love you."

Quindlen advises us not to waste our days, our hours, and our minutes. To think of life as a terminal illness, because if we do, we'll live it each day with gusto, joy, and passion. If we do that, we'll cherish the journey, not just the destination. We'll live life the way it was meant to be lived—with each day being a gift. Perhaps the greatest gift of all is the gift of time, time for a sick friend, time to mentor, time to share, and time to love.

Let's take time out for a moment and talk about another gift we need to give ourselves and that's "time off." We need to take quality time for ourselves. It's important to re-charge our batteries once in a while. We tend to brag about not taking a vacation and keeping our nose to the grindstone. But it's vitally important to take time off for both you and your family. Ultimately, it's good for your company too—because your mind will be more refreshed, allowing you to see things more clearly upon your return. The net result is often better creativity and productivity.

*Know the value of time; snatch, seize and enjoy every moment of it. No idleness, no laziness, no procrastination. Never put off till tomorrow what you can do today.*
—CHESTERFIELD

## Time Is Fleeting

Time is one thing we cannot recycle. I don't mean to be morbid, but we have only so much time left in our lives. In fact, if one were to divide an average lifetime into thirds, many baby boomers born between the mid-1940s and early 1960s are already approaching the last third of their lives. Now stay with me on this, and I'll make it come alive for you. In fact, let's try to boil our life down to heartbeats.

- If a person lives to an average age of seventy-five years old, he will have more than 3 billion heartbeats in his lifetime. That's an average of 40 million heartbeats in a year.

- At fifty-five years old this person has approximately 800 million heartbeats left in his life . . . or about 27 percent of all the heartbeats in his entire lifetime.

- At forty-five years old, this person has approximately 1.2 billion heartbeats left in his life . . . or about 40 percent of all the heartbeats in his lifetime.

- At thirty-five years old, this person has approximately 1.6 billion heartbeats left in his life . . . or about 54 percent of all the heartbeats in his lifetime.

We have only a limited number of heartbeats. It's up to us to decide how to use them. Andy Rooney summed it up best when he said, "Life is like a roll of toilet paper— the closer it gets to the end, the faster it goes!" Too many of us realize the importance of time only when we have very little of it left.

There's a great story that author Jeffrey Davis tells in his book *1,000 Marbles*. A fifty-five-year-old person has about a thousand Saturdays left to live in their lifetime (provided they live to be seventy-five years old). To commemorate this he suggests that we go out and buy one thousand marbles (or pieces of candy for that matter) and place them in a clear plastic container. Every Saturday take one marble out and throw it away. When you watch your marbles diminish, you can more readily focus on the important things in life.

There's nothing like watching your time here on this earth run out to help you focus on what really matters most. By the way, what are you doing this Saturday? Going out to dinner? Playing on the beach with your kids? Taking in a great movie? Inviting some close friends over for a barbecue? Make every day count—especially Saturdays. Ask yourself this question: When was the last time you did something that you've never experienced before?

Time is one resource we cannot regenerate. The message rings out clearly. Spend time; invest your time now on things that matter most to you. Don't wait to take that romantic trip to Venice, Italy. Don't wait to tell your kids you love them. Don't wait until you're too old to enjoy trekking the foothills of the Himalayas. Don't wait to buy that house next to the babbling brook. Don't wait to start your own company. Your time is now!

## EXECUTIVE SUMMARY

Chapter nine centers on the distribution part of the marketing-plan process. In business, distribution is about being selective as to where you sell your product or service. You are not likely to see Tiffany being sold at the jewelry section of Wal-Mart. In business circles you are often judged by the company you keep. Distribution is also about efficiency and time management.

On a personal level, we're talking about spending quality time with quality people. It's not just about time management—it's about quality time management. It's about spending and investing your time wisely pursuing your true purpose in life. It's not about spreading yourself so thin you can't focus on the things that matter most in your life. We're reminded to spend time with people who send off positive energy, people who encourage us to fulfill our goals, dreams, and aspirations.

The chapter concludes with a dose of reality. Time is fleeting. Time is one resource we can't regenerate. The message is crystal clear: Spend time now on that which matters most to you.

## EXERCISE 1: DISTRIBUTING YOUR TIME WISELY

Before we can distribute our time more wisely, we need to hone in on what really matters most to us. We need to know what we want to make time for. Accordingly, check off the things on this list that you wish were a bigger part of your life:

__ Overall family fun

__ Son

__ Daughter

__ Wife

__ Husband

__ Niece/nephew

__ Granddaughter/ grandson

__ Relationships

__ Career

__ New career

__ Health

__ Quality leisure time (travel, etc.)

__ Hobbies (specify)

__ Education/self-education

__ Community/ volunteer work

__ Managing your personal portfolio

__ Getting more in touch with nature

__ Your home or vacation home

__ Sports: golf, tennis, mountain climbing, working out, etc.

__ Other (please specify)

_____

_____

_____

_____

## EXERCISE 2: INVESTING TIME ON WHAT MATTERS MOST

Now that you've discovered what you want to make time for, it's time for you to fill out your own pie charts. Remember each slice of the pie should represent a percent value as to what matters most to you.

### HOW DO YOU WISH YOU WERE SPENDING YOUR TIME?

### HOW ARE YOU CURRENTLY SPENDING YOUR TIME?

## EXERCISE 3: INVESTING YOUR TIME WISELY

A.  If you knew you had only six months to live, would you spend your time more wisely in the following areas? Would you make any changes? Please explain:

1. Family _____

_____

_____

2. Relationships _____

_____

_____

3. Leisure time/travel _____

_____

_____

4. Financial portfolio or will _____

_____

_____

5. Career or profession _____

_____

_____

6. Community or charitable work _____

_____

_____

7. Other: Please specify _____

_____

_____

_____

_____

B.  If you knew a loved one (a spouse, family member, or friend) had only six months to live, describe how you would treat them in their remaining days.

Why not treat them that way right now?

_____

_____

_____

_____

_____

C.  If you had only one hour to live, who would you call and what would you say?

_____

_____

_____

_____

What are you waiting for?

TIME TO REFLECT

*Are you currently spending quality time on those things that matter most to you?*

# CHAPTER 10

# ACHIEVE YOUR SALES GOALS

## Reaching Out to Make Your Personal Goals a Reality

*Goals are dreams with deadlines.*
—DIANA SCHARF-HUNT

The next point in the marketing-plan process is sales. On the business front, we have to sell our products, services, programs, concepts, and even an idea or two occasionally. To paraphrase Arthur H. "Red" Motley, former publisher of *Parade* magazine, nothing really happens in business or, come to think of it, in life until somebody sells something. Even a starving artist has to sell something, sometime! Most of all, we have to sell ourselves in order to make things happen.

In our business or professional lives, we live in a world where setting goals and sales targets are an integral part of running a business. It is not uncommon for sales people to have weekly and monthly sales goals, quarterly sales targets, and annual sales reviews. Good companies review these goals for validity each quarter, at the very least. Business goals are often readjusted to conform to the swings or moods of the marketplace.

Sales people recognize that goal setting is "business as usual." In the corporate sales world it's a commonplace way to monitor progress. Those who sell also understand the importance of reaching their goals. Hitting goals and exceeding them is often linked to higher commissions, sales bonuses, or even promotions.

Most people easily set goals in their business or professional life, but many don't take the time to set goals in their personal lives. To achieve a life that offers personal fulfillment and meaning, it is important that we focus on *personal* goals as well as professional goals. Our personal goals are the signposts we need to steer in the right direction and to begin to see the light at the end of the tunnel.

But your personal goals should not be cast in concrete. Just like the ever-changing business marketplace, there could be events in your personal life that cause you to consider adjusting your goals. As in setting business goals, it may be wise to revisit your personal goals every six months. Setting personal goals will help you concentrate not only on "what" you want to achieve, but "when" you want to achieve them.

## Goals Versus Objectives

It really surprises me that most people don't know the difference between an objective and a goal. An objective is general in nature—for instance, *I'd like to lose weight*. A goal, however, is always, always, always quantifiable—it has numbers and time attached to it. A goal is, *I'd like to lose ten pounds in the next six weeks and keep that weight off forever*.

Here are a few examples of personal goals to get you off and running:

- I'd like to enter and finish the Los Angeles Marathon next year.
- I'd like to take eight months off and sail around the world starting next winter.
- I'd like to have a baby within two years.
- I'd like to increase my financial portfolio by 10 percent this year.
- I'd like to start a new marketing consulting business over the next eighteen months.

It's important that we understand that achieving our personal goals, dreams, and aspirations is inexorably linked to meeting our professional goals. In fact, they're literally joined at the hip. For example, I may want to buy a new house or new car, but it will take me a lot longer if I don't meet my business goals, or increase my stock portfolio, or receive my year-end bonus, or earn that commission check. Adding a new baby to the family might require more income in order to maintain your existing lifestyle.

## Focusing on Goals

Once you define and quantify your personal goals, you need to stay focused on achieving them. Here are some action steps that will allow you to stay focused on your goals:

1. **Write them down.** First and foremost, write your goals down. You can write them down in the back of a daily planner, or in a separate book that you can readily access on a daily basis. Clear, well-written goals are the basic staple of high achievers. A study of Harvard graduates found that after twenty years, the 3 percent of graduates who had recorded their goals in writing went on to achieve more financial success than the other 97 percent combined.

2. **Put them where you can see them.** Place your written goals or picture of the end result on your refrigerator or another highly visible place. It might be an inspirational quote that reaffirms your commitment to achieving your goals.

3. **Recite daily affirmations.** Each day, repeat an affirmation statement consistent with attaining your goal. For example: "Today I will continue to move toward the completion of my book."

4. **Go public.** Tell someone whom you respect or admire that you are in the process of achieving a goal. It puts some pressure on you, but it also focuses you on the task at hand. It also adds to your support group.

5. **Use poignant symbols.** Place symbols of your end goal in your office or in your house. For example, if you want to move to Big Sur, show a picture of the waves crashing against the region's distinctive coastline. If you want to take a trip to Italy, then find a picture to inspire you to actually take the trip.

6. **Visualize success.** See yourself succeeding by making mental rehearsals. Try visualizing yourself achieving your goal in your mind's eye long before it actually happens.

*Never judge a sailor on a calm sea.*

—OLD IRISH EXPRESSION

## Sales and Perseverance

The sales process has a lot to do with perseverance. Perseverance is often the key difference in separating those who achieve versus those who do not. Our tenacity allows us to overcome adversity and the choppy waters that the storms of life present to us. As mentioned earlier, my mother always echoed the old Irish expression, "Never judge a sailor on a calm sea."

One of my favorite tales of perseverance and tenacity involves the building of the Brooklyn Bridge. In his award-winning book *The Great Bridge*, author David McCullough chronicles the twenty years of effort it took to build this architectural masterpiece.

Before the building of the bridge, the trip across the East River from Manhattan to Brooklyn was an arduous one—there were just too many boats on the water in the summer months, and during the frozen winter the trip became nearly impossible. In 1863, engineer John A. Roebling drafted plans for a bridge. Although Roebling had a great reputation as a bridge engineer, many reputable engineers doubted that the bridge could be built. Others thought that the bridge's innovative suspension design would sway too much in heavy winds.

Finally in 1869, President Grant approved the plans to build the Brooklyn Bridge. However, a month later, John Roebling died from complications stemming from an accident. His son, Colonel Washington Roebling, took over as chief engineer. By then, political corruption added to the skepticism that the bridge could even be built. In 1872, after some real progress, Washington Roebling was struck with decompression illness, which occurs due to the high pressure in the bridge construction's underwater enclosures. The disease rendered him partially paralyzed. He also lost the use of his voice. It was then that his wife, Emily, began assisting him as her husband watched construction of the bridge through his bedroom window. Later, Emily took complete charge of the project and saw the completion of the bridge in 1883. When the bridge finally opened in 1883, it was heralded as one of the most magnificent construction projects of the nineteenth century. Now that's perseverance!

> *Let me tell you the secret that has led me to my goal:*
> *My strength lies solely in my tenacity.*
> —LOUIS PASTEUR

We've all had moments in our lives when we had to call on our powers of perseverance. As the senior marketing vice president of an eyewear company, I tried to reach a licensing agreement with Laura Ashley Limited for Laura Ashley Eyewear—and was turned down more than twenty times! Then one day, I sent a fax to the company's London headquarters telling them that I was going to be in England with my partner and would like to see them concerning the potential licensing deal. After conducting our initial business in London, we went out for a quick pint at a London pub. It was time to head over to Laura Ashley's headquarters. But my partner, who is a kindhearted soul, took a wrinkled fax from Laura Ashley out of his attaché case. It read, "Dear Mr. Fried, Thanks for informing us of your intent to come to London. Don't come now. Don't come ever. Don't come. We're not interested."

Undeterred, I said, "Let's go anyway." After all, we were already in London. We were taken on a one-hour taxi ride by a crafty cabbie, not knowing that Laura Ashley's corporate headquarters was only five minutes away from the pub. But that one-hour delay allowed us to catch Laura Ashley's managing director, who was in the office late burning the midnight oil. In the meeting we convinced him that we could create incremental licensing revenues while protecting the integrity of the brand. That impromptu meeting led us to closing one of the biggest business licensing deals of my career. That success had nothing to do with being smart—it had everything to do with perseverance.

*If people see themselves as a person they can become, and act as if they are that person, soon they will not be acting.*
—CYNTHIA KERSEY

## Visualize Success

An essential part of succeeding in the selling process is putting yourself in the proper mind-set to succeed. Sales motivation experts suggest that in order to reach a goal, you must visualize the end result. Literally, you must "see" the reaching in your own mind before you actually arrive at your goal. People who succeed often make "mental rehearsals"—they script themselves for success. That's why you often see Olympic downhill skiers using "creative visualization," seeing themselves perfectly executing each gate on their way to a gold medal. Top-selling real-estate brokers visualize the "sold" sign going up. (However, the best brokers see themselves already spending their commission check on a shiny new car!) Likewise, highly trained karate experts visualize the end result by "seeing through the brick" on their way to smashing it in half.

Sometimes, the ability to "see" the end goal is the difference between success and failure. In the 1950s, endurance swimmer Florence Chadwick set a goal for herself that was going to be tough to meet. She was already the first woman to swim the English Channel in both directions. Now, at age thirty-four, her goal was to become the first woman to swim from Catalina Island to the California coast. On that Fourth of July morning in 1952, the sea was like an ice bath and the fog was so dense she could hardly see her support boats. Looking ahead, Florence saw nothing but a thick wall of fog. Her body was numb from the cold. She had been swimming for nearly sixteen hours. Sharks cruised toward her, only to be chased away by rifle shots. Against the current of the icy, choppy sea, she struggled on while millions watched on national television.

Alongside Florence in one of the boats, her mother and her trainer offered shouts of encouragement. They urged her on by telling her she didn't have much farther to swim. But all Florence could see was a dense layer of fog. Florence was not known for being a quitter. But with only about a half mile to go, she asked to be pulled out of the freezing water. After thawing out her body she told a reporter, "Look, I'm not excusing myself, but if I could have seen land I might have made it." It was not fatigue or even the icy water that defeated her. It was the fog that blocked her vision. She was unable to see her goal.

Two months later, she tried the same swim again. This time, despite the same thick fog, she swam with her focus intact and her goal clearly pictured in her mind. She knew that somewhere behind that fog was land and her goal. Not surprisingly, this time she made it! Florence Chadwick became the first woman to swim the Catalina Channel, eclipsing the men's record at the time by two hours. Her mantra: Even if you can't "see" the end of your journey, always keep your goals in sight.

*The arrow that hits bull's-eye is the result of one hundred misses.*
—AN OLD ADAGE

There are many other classic examples of why we shouldn't give up. Take a look at this litany of people who never quit:

- Winston Churchill was the odds-on favorite to become prime minister in his early thirties, but did not secure the position until age sixty-six.

- TV soap-opera actress Susan Lucci finally won her coveted Emmy in 1999 after having lost eighteen times in her bid to garner the award.

- Colin Powell got his first job mopping floors at a Pepsi-Cola bottling company.

- Kurt Warner, NFL quarterback and Most Valuable Player, worked as a grocery-store bagger shortly before joining the St. Louis Rams and winning the Super Bowl.

- Albert Einstein was four years old before he spoke and seven before he could read.

- Ludwig van Beethoven's music teacher once said of him, "As a composer, he is hopeless."

- Thomas Edison failed more than four thousand times before he invented the lightbulb.

- A newspaper editor fired Walt Disney because he "lacked creativity."

- Ted Turner was expelled from college.

- Louis Pasteur was rated as "mediocre" in chemistry by his professors at the Royal College.

- As a young student, Martin Luther King Jr. was told by a teacher that he would never be able to speak with enough passion to inspire people to take action.

*Ah, but a man's reach should exceed his grasp, or what's a heaven for?*
—ROBERT BROWNING

## Think Big!

When it comes to sales, we have to think big. My mentor always reminded me, "It's just as easy to sell a cabin cruiser as it is a canoe! Customers ask the same two questions: 'How much is it?' and 'Is it going to sink?'" It takes the same amount of effort, but the reward for selling a cabin cruiser is greater than selling a canoe, so don't be afraid to reach out and work on the big things. Go after the big fish!

FedEx chairman and CEO Fred Smith is the very personification of one who thinks big. He also knew how to sell himself. While a student at Yale, Smith wrote a term paper proposing a unique global freight and package delivery system. He thought the behemoth U.S. Postal Service was ripe for the taking. Smith was right. He created FedEx, which is today the world's largest package-delivery company. One of the proudest moments in Smith's career came when the U.S. Postal Service decided to add FedEx drop boxes in post offices around the country. Fred Smith succeeded because he had a big vision and was willing to take the necessary risks to make his vision a reality. But the primary reason he succeeded is that he wasn't afraid to fail. He wasn't afraid to take on the vulnerable U.S. Postal Service.

*Success is not built on success. It is built on failure.*
—SUMNER REDSTONE

High-achieving people are not afraid to fail. They consider their mistakes as only temporary setbacks or stepping-stones on the road to achieving their goals. Failures are inevitable. Failures indicate a willingness to reach out and take risks. People who achieve their dreams know that failure brings them another step closer to realizing their goal.

In her engaging book *Unstoppable*, Cynthia Kersey says that it's through failure that we ultimately achieve our goals. "Being able to see failure as an opportunity for learning and improvement is critical to becoming unstoppable. People who can't bear a moment of failure have doomed themselves to mediocrity, for they'll never be able to push themselves past a point that is uncomfortable or unfamiliar. Yet it is beyond that place where success dwells."

An important part of the selling process is not being afraid to fail. Think of it, Major League Baseball batters go to the Hall of Fame by failing two-out-of-three times! Do the math: You get one hit for every three times at bat, your average is .333, and you're on your way to Cooperstown. At one time, Babe Ruth held records for the most home runs but also the most strikeouts. In fact, when a reporter asked The Babe what he thought about when he struck out, Ruth said, "That's easy. I think about hitting home runs."

## If at First You Don't Succeed . . .

Sometimes the best stories of persistence and perseverance reside right in your own family. By the time my nephew reached college, Kevin already knew what he wanted to do in life. He wanted to help people with their pain. He wanted to be a doctor.

Although Kevin got good grades in college, he didn't do well when he initially took the Medical College Admission Test (MCAT). He was very disappointed, but decided to get his master's in neuroscience to be in better position to reapply to medical school. Once again, Kevin failed to achieve a good score on the MCAT exam. Kevin was disconsolate, but refused to give up. He decided to take a job as a medical researcher with the idea that he'd give medical school one last try. But once again, he failed to pass his MCAT exam. No medical school in the country would accept him.

Still unwavering, Kevin decided to apply to a small medical school in the Caribbean Islands. Finally, he was accepted to medical school. Kevin's plan was bold: Get straight A's in the small medical school in the Caribbean and eventually work his way back to a good residency position in the United States.

Kevin worked hard in the small foreign medical school and graduated near the top of his class. He applied to many U.S. schools for his residency, but highly respected Stanford was his top choice. There was one small problem: Stanford very rarely accepted foreign students into their program.

During his interview at Stanford, Kevin's quest to get into their residency program, against all odds, struck a respondent chord with his interviewers. They recognized that great doctors know more than medicine—they also understand life and overcoming adversity. They all came to the same conclusion: Stanford needed doctors like Kevin. He was unanimously admitted to one of the best residency programs in the country—ten years after his med school odyssey began.

In summary, failure is just another pit stop on the road to success. All of us are going to fail at times. But we can't permit fear of failure to stymie our efforts to reach our goal. We cannot deprive ourselves from being all we can be. As legendary UCLA basketball coach John Wooden said, "The man who is afraid to risk failure seldom has to face success."

## EXECUTIVE SUMMARY

This chapter points out that nothing really happens in business or in life until somebody sells something. In order to make things happen we need to not only sell ourselves but also to set personal goals that can be quantified. Achieving your business goals is often linked at the hip with making your personal goals a reality. Perseverance is often the key difference in separating those who achieve versus those who do not.

Another key element in the selling process is not being afraid to fail. The lessons of failure often lead to success. Remember, the arrow that hits the bull's-eye is the result of one hundred misses.

## EXERCISE 1: WRITE DOWN YOUR GOALS

Write down your major short-term goals (one to two years out) and your major long-term goals (three to five years out). Remember, goals are always quantifiable: They have numbers and time attached to them (for example, "lose ten pounds in ten weeks"). Be sure to reevaluate your goals at least every six months by the categories listed below:

### FAMILY GOALS

A. Short term (one to two years from today)

(Example: Spend one weekend per month with my aging parents)

1. _____
2. _____
3. _____

B. Long term (three to five years from today)

(Example: Take my family on trips of learning and discovery to Europe and Asia)

1. _____
2. _____
3. _____

### HEALTH GOALS

A. Short term (one to two years from today)

(Example: Lose ten pounds in year one, another five pounds in year two)

1. _____
2. _____
3. _____

B.  Long term (three to five years from today)

(Example: Maintain a cholesterol level below 200)

1.  _____

2.  _____

3.  _____


## CAREER/PROFESSIONAL GOALS

A.  Short term (one to two years from today)

(Example: Become my company's sales director in year one and vice president of sales in year two)

1.  _____

2.  _____

3.  _____

B.  Long term (three to five years from today)

(Example: Start my own business in the area of personal growth and grow the business by 20 percent each year)

1.  _____

2.  _____

3.  _____


## FINANCIAL GOALS

A.  Short term (one to two years from today)

(Example: Increase my personal portfolio by 10 percent each year)

1.  _____

2.  _____

3.  _____

B.  Long term (three to five years from today)

(Example: To buy a vacation home in Carmel, California, no later than year three)

1. _____

2. _____

3. _____


## RELATIONSHIP GOALS

A.  Short term (one to two years from today)

(Example: Spend more quality time with my family and closest friends versus my business acquaintances)

1. _____

2. _____

3. _____

B.  Long term (three to five years from today)

(Example: I'd like to be married and start a family)

1. _____

2. _____

3. _____


## PERSONAL GROWTH GOALS

A.  Short term (one to two years from today)

(Example: Identify my true purpose and passion in life and take action to identify what really matters most to me)

1. _____

2. _____

3. _____

B. Long term (three to five years from today)

**(Example: Write a book in the area of personal growth)**

    1. _____

    2. _____

    3. _____

## LEISURE TIME AND TRAVEL GOALS

A. Short term (one to two years from today)

**(Example: Play golf once a week)**

    1. _____

    2. _____

    3. _____

B. Long term (three to five years from today)

**(Example: Take a month off to tour Italy and Spain)**

    1. _____

    2. _____

    3. _____

## MISCELLANEOUS GOALS (THINGS I ALWAYS WANTED TO DO)

A. Short term (one to two years from today)

**(Example: Learn to play the guitar)**

    1. _____

    2. _____

    3. _____

B. Long term (three to five years from today)

   (Example: Climb Mount Rainier)

   1. _____

   2. _____

   3. _____


## EXERCISE 2: PERSEVERANCE

List the times in your life when you persevered to achieve your goals. How did you feel when you stayed focused and succeeded?

_____

_____

_____


## EXERCISE 3: FEAR OF FAILURE

List the times in your life when fear of failure stymied you in your efforts to achieve your purpose or business goals. What would you have done differently?

_____

_____

_____


### TIME TO REFLECT

*Has fear of failure stymied your efforts to achieve your personal or business goals?*

# CHAPTER 11

# ANALYZE THE PROFIT AND LOSS
## Tallying Your Personal Balance Sheet

*Those who stand for nothing fall for anything.*
—ALEXANDER HAMILTON

Profitability is a company's just reward for having properly executed the preceding points of the marketing-plan discipline. Profitability creates value for a company, its employees, and its stockholders. Profit is what puts food on the table and creates year-end bonuses.

In recent years, it has become a bit tougher to discern when a company is truly profitable. In January 2001, Enron announced record financial and operating results for the previous year. In a press release, Enron's chairman and CEO, Kenneth L. Lay, remarked, "Our strong results reflect breakout performances in all of our operations. Our wholesale services, retail energy and broadband businesses further expanded their leading market positions, as reflected in record levels of physical deliveries, contract originations and profitability." Less than twelve months later, the company filed for bankruptcy.

In 2000, WorldCom reported a profit of $4 billion. By 2001, its reported profits had dropped to $1.4 billion. By 2003, the company was in bankruptcy.

When Tyco's CEO, L. Dennis Kozlowski, announced his company's financial results for 2000, he said, "Tyco continues to show no signs of slowing down. Organic growth remained strong across the board. We continued to expand our operating margins to record levels." You know the rest of the story.

These were all large, respected companies. Their financial results had been audited by internationally recognized accounting firms. Their shares belonged in the core holdings of the most sophisticated money managers in the nation. Yet something was amiss.

If we investigate the celebrated corporate meltdowns of the last several years, there are companies that failed (or refused) to answer financial questions in an accurate, straightforward way. Companies that hide liabilities off the balance sheet or ship empty boxes to boost reported sales are simply dodging the fundamental questions that financial statements are designed to answer. A hodgepodge of extraordinary gains and charges, accounting changes and restatements more often disguise a company's true value than reveal them.

Today, companies that are admired and held in high esteem not only report accurately, but just as important, they truly value their core values. Great companies don't just hang their core value beliefs on the wall—they live by them day by day. This corporate consciousness is one of the things that makes a good company a great company.

## Your Personal Balance Sheet

Let's talk about your personal balance sheet for Me, Inc. Your personal balance sheet has a lot to do with having a good value system. Good values enhance our self-equity and self-worth. Bad ethics or values will lower our sense of self-worth and self-esteem. We as individuals can all profit from a good value system. As mentioned in earlier chapters, a key element of knowing yourself is determining that which matters most to you. A good value system lays the foundation for those things that you stand for and truly believe in. Our good values will often determine how we act in a given situation, especially in turbulent times—times when life seems to be moving too rapidly or closing in on us. Our good values will provide the core stabilization we need to make life's choices based on our authentic sense of self-worth. According to management consultant Jim Clemmer our core values provide us with a stronger sense of personal bottom line. Says Clemmer, "Knowing where we stand on things clarifies what we won't stand for."

*A people that values its privileges above its principles soon loses both.*

—DWIGHT D. EISENHOWER

## The Pressure to Create Value Leads to Scandal

Companies were under more pressure than ever to create shareholder value. Some tried to do so by reporting profits that seemed to increase quarter by quarter, minute by minute. As each hurdle grew higher than the one before it, some managers were tempted first to manage earnings, then to invent them. The bottom line: Deceit and nondisclosure ultimately resulted in a plummeting stock price for companies like Enron and WorldCom.

Investors have realized that companies with good business ethics and honest reporting are likely a better bet for their investment dollar. In fact, for public companies the guidelines for financial reporting have changed, requiring company executives to personally vouch for the numbers they report to the public. More than ever, good business ethics add to the overall value of a company in much the same way as profitability and growth. Clearly, questionable business ethics can significantly decrease a company's value and stock price.

*If you tell the truth, you don't have to remember anything.*

—MARK TWAIN

Jerome Kohlberg Jr., from the private equity firm of Kohlberg, Kravis, Roberts and Company, addressed the breakdown of values in corporate America: "All around us there is a breakdown of values. It is not just the overpowering greed that pervades our business life. It is the fact that we are not willing to sacrifice for the ethics and values we profess. For an ethic is not an ethic, and a value is not a value, without some sacrifice to it. Something given up, something not taken, something not gained."

## All Companies Are Not the Same

Enron, Arthur Andersen, and WorldCom are just three of what was a rash of spectacular corporate scandals in the late 1990s. These companies undermined confidence in the stock market and launched a populist wave of support for corporate reform—including greater accountability and calls for lower top management pay. But for every Enron or World-

Com, there are many more honest companies that take disclosure and accountability as seriously as they do making money. And in many cases, these companies succeed on all fronts. More often than not, the most admired companies on the business landscape are profitable. They also, year after year, answer profit and loss questions in an accurate, straightforward way. *Forbes* magazine compiles an annual list of the most admired companies and here (as of this writing) are a few examples from that list.

### Procter & Gamble

P&G is America's number-one maker of household products, with offerings in five categories: fabric and home care, beauty care, baby and family care, health care, plus snacks and beverages. The firm also makes pet food and water filters, and even produces two soap operas: *Guiding Light* and *As the World Turns*. Thirteen of P&G's brands are billion-dollar sellers, including Always/Whisper, Ariel, Bounty, Charmin, Crest, Downy/Lenor, Folgers, Iams, Olay, Pampers, Pantene, Pringles, and Tide. This company clearly knows how to manage brands and produce a return on investment for its shareholders. But the company also takes great effort to maintain a high corporate character. Its purpose statement reads as follows: "P&G people are committed to serving consumers and achieving leadership results through principle-based decisions and actions." There are similar statements within the company's core values on leadership, ownership, passion for winning, trust, and integrity. The company's adherence to these solid core values has made it one of the most admired companies in America.

### Johnson & Johnson

Johnson & Johnson is one of the world's largest, most diversified health-care product makers with three main sectors. Its consumer products segment makes over-the-counter drugs and products for skin and hair care, baby care, oral care, first aid, and women's health and nutrition. The company's medical devices and diagnostics division includes such products as surgical equipment, medical monitoring devices, and disposable contact lenses. Finally, J&J's largest segment, pharmaceuticals, makes drugs for a vast array of aliments, including heart disease, oncology, and pain management. Top brands include household names like Tylenol and Band-Aid.

While many companies have mission statements that gather dust hanging on the wall, Johnson & Johnson has a simple one-page credo that has remained unchanged for more than fifty years. This venerable credo has served to guide the company's actions in fulfilling responsibilities to customers, employees, the community, and stockholders. It begins with responsibilities to the doctors, nurses, and patients who use the company's products and services. Then it goes on to list responsibilities to employees, the communities, and the stockholders: "Business must make a sound profit. We must experiment with new ideas. Research must be carried on, innovative programs developed and mistakes paid for. New equipment must be purchased, new facilities provided and new products launched. Reserves must be created to provide for adverse times. When we operate according to these principles, the stockholders should realize a fair return." With words like this providing guidance for more than fifty years, it is no wonder that the company is both profitable and admired.

## Berkshire Hathaway

Financial institutions seemed to fare the worst in the fallout of corporate scandals. Credit Suisse First Boston and others were suspected of misleading investors and brokering unfair transactions for larger customers. But Berkshire Hathaway remains an admired and profitable company. Led by majority owner Warren Buffett, the company operates in the insurance industry and uses the "float"—the cash collected before claims are paid out—to invest in a growing stable of businesses. But the numbers tell a better story: In 2002, the company grew 13.3 percent, with a net income growth of 439 percent. As one of the most admired companies in America, they experienced a 33 percent growth in employees in 2002.

To articulate the company's commitment to profitability and values, Berkshire Hathaway offers an "Owner's Manual" to all shareholders. The purpose of the manual is to explain the company's broad economic principles of operation. In very plain language it manages to accomplish this. The document includes a strong statement on partnership, spoken in the first person by Buffet, the company's chairman: "Although our form is corporate, our attitude is partnership. Charlie Munger and I think of our shareholders as owner-partners, and of ourselves as managing partners. (Because of the size of our shareholdings we are also, for better or worse, controlling partners.) We do not view the company itself as the ultimate owner of our business assets but instead view the company as a conduit through which our shareholders own the assets."

There is also a candid statement about each shareholder visualizing themselves as a "part owner of a business that you expect to stay with indefinitely." Finally, there is a very frank statement on sharing the risk and benefits of their business: "In line with Berkshire's owner-orientation, most of our directors have a major portion of their net worth invested in the company. We eat our own cooking."

Berkshire Hathaway has managed to put these words into action, and in a very volatile industry, remain a trusted and profitable company.

## Identifying Our Core Values

Just like these successful businesses, it's crucial that each one of us take the time to identify and later clarify our core values. Says my esteemed colleague Dr. Dan Baker, "When we identify these values it gives our life focus and a sense of security—especially during times of chaos and confusion."

Take a look at the core values listed below and on the next page. Mentally or physically, check off those core values that apply most to you. Later in the workbook exercise section of the chapter, you'll have an opportunity to narrow down your list.

| | | |
|---|---|---|
| __ Accomplishments | __ Dedication | __ Family |
| __ Adventure | __ Dependability | __ Fitness |
| __ Aggressiveness | __ Design | __ Flexibility |
| __ Art | __ Devotion | __ Freedom |
| __ Authenticity | __ Direction | __ Faithfulness |
| __ Beauty | __ Discovery | __ Fun |
| __ Bravery | __ Dream fulfillment | __ Generosity |
| __ Business | __ Education | __ Gifts |
| __ Causes | __ Empathy | __ Greatness |
| __ Charity | __ Encouragement | __ Guidance |
| __ Comfort | __ Energy | __ Happiness |
| __ Community | __ Enrichment | __ Hard work |
| __ Compassion | __ Ethics | __ Health |
| __ Connectedness | __ Excellence | __ Helpfulness |
| __ Control | __ Exhilaration | __ Honesty |
| __ Courage | __ Fairness | __ Honor |
| __ Creativity | __ Faith | __ Humility |

| | | |
|---|---|---|
| __ Humor | __ Mentorship | __ Simplicity |
| __ Imagination | __ Moving forward | __ Spirituality |
| __ Information | __ Open-minded | __ Spontaneity |
| __ Ingenuity | __ Originality | __ Sports |
| __ Inspiration | __ Outspokenness | __ Strength |
| __ Integrity | __ Patience | __ Support |
| __ Intelligence | __ Peace | __ Thoughtfulness |
| __ Inventiveness | __ People | __ Trust |
| __ Joy | __ Perceptiveness | __ Truth |
| __ Kindness | __ Perseverance | __ Turning Points |
| __ Lack of bigotry | __ Persuasion | __ Understanding |
| __ Lack of racism | __ Planning | __ Uniqueness |
| __ Laughter | __ Providing | __ Uplifting |
| __ Learning | __ The quest | __ Wealth |
| __ Logic | __ Religion | __ What really matters most |
| __ Love | __ Reverence | |
| __ Loyalty | __ Right risks | __ Winning |
| __ Making a difference | __ Romance | __ Wisdom |
| | __ Security | |
| __ Making an impact | __ Serenity | |

## Values Steer You in the Right Direction

Identifying and clarifying your core values gives you a virtual road map that will guide you in making key decisions as you travel through the journey of life. Our values act as a compass that leads you in the right direction and steers you back on course.

When you live up to your core values, you begin to focus in on a much clearer sense of purpose—one that is aligned with the authentic you. As Roy Disney once said, "It's not hard to make decisions when you know what your values are."

As this 2001 study indicates, Americans today are increasingly moving back to core values. Let's take a look at the chart below:

| WHAT WAS | WHAT IS |
|---|---|
| Whatever | What matters |
| Getting by | Getting a life |
| About me | About community |
| Trying to do it all | Making choices |
| Learning to invest | Keeping/giving away |
| Lone wolf | Mentors |
| Working vacations | Long vacations |

Source: Roper Starch Worldwide 2001

When one considers the world events of the past several years, the research above is particularly valid today. In the past several years, we've gone through the dot-com bust, steep stock market declines, significant layoffs, the horror of 9/11, corporate and Wall Street deceit, church child abuse scandals, continued terrorist threats, and war in the Middle East. It's a good bet that by the time this book goes to press you could add a few more worldwide events that will continue to move us closer to our core set of values.

## Forming Your Value System

How we formulate our value system has always been the subject of varied opinion. According to many experts, our value system is formed at an early age, often between eight and twelve years old. That's why you often hear someone who grew up during the breadlines and the Depression of the 1930s say security-conscious things like:

"Save a penny for a rainy day."

"Eat everything on your plate. There are poor people starving around the world."

"What do you mean . . . you're a senior in college and you still don't know what you want to be yet?"

However, their boomer kids (born between 1946 and 1962) are likely to be far less security minded than their Depression-era parents. Why? Boomers are accustomed to challenging existing institutions and old ideas. Questioning the notion of traditional rocking-chair retirement is no exception. It is very likely that boomers will demand much more than tee times and bingo in their retirement years. The boomer generation seeks experience and discovery as much as the financial security that was often the chief concern of their parents.

Dr. Dan Baker reminds us that our values can change as we grow older and go through the winds or passages of life. Here's a chart Baker used at our Marketing Plan for Life seminar.

| AGE | SOURCE OF VALUES |
| --- | --- |
| 6–8 | Family |
| 8–12 | Heroes |
| 12–20 | Peers |
| 21 and over | Life's experiences |

Looking at his chart and considering my own life, I'd say that Dr. Baker is definitely onto something here. When I was 6 to 8 years old, my mother was the primary influence in my life, simply because my dad worked long hours at his restaurant. My fiery, red-haired Irish Catholic mother didn't always agree with my dark-haired Jewish father. But they did agree on important things—because they had the same good, solid value system. They taught us at an early age to respect people of various races and religious beliefs. I believe that these core values instilled at an early age helped me immensely in building the international segment of my business because I was alertly attuned to racial, cultural, and religious nuances that helped me later in life to market effectively to other countries.

From ages 8 to 12, I worshiped my baseball hero Mickey Mantle and idolized the New York Yankees. If the Yankees lost or Mantle went hitless, it could literally ruin my day. (I know a lot of you had similar feelings when it came to worshiping your childhood heros.)

Between the ages of 12 and 20, I guess I was not unlike most of us—I wanted to fit in so I joined various clubs and fraternities to be one of the guys. In the years that followed, my twenty-first birthday, I was definitely influenced by my life's experiences from college to various management positions, to my parents' recent deaths, to the fast-paced and ever-changing world events. When I stop and think about it, this book itself is greatly influenced and is a natural outgrowth of my life's experiences and core value system. But as someone once said, "My ultimate goal is to be as good a person as my dog already thinks I am."

## Balancing Your Personal Integrity Account

Each time you act in accordance with your core values, you essentially make deposits in what authors A. Roger Merrill and Rebecca R. Merrill call your "Personal Integrity Account." This, they point out, is your most important trust account because it reflects the amount of trust you have in your relationship with your authentic self. The more you stay within your core value system, the more you act on what really matters most—the more you deposit into your personal account. The more this account is balanced with core values, the more likely you are to feel a sense of high self-esteem and self-worth.

> *The time is always right to do what is right.*
> —MARTIN LUTHER KING JR.

My personal sense of self-worth was never higher than when I quit an excellent job because, although the job was a lucrative one, the company's values weren't compatible with my own.

One spring, my boss asked me to hire an MBA marketing major from one of the country's top business schools as a summer intern. Let's call this intern Adam. But my boss threw me what I considered to be an unethical knuckleball. He wanted me to lure Adam to the company for the summer (to help out with a big project) by promising a full-time position—then fire him at the end of the summer, regardless of his job performance. I objected strongly to this proposal, to which my boss replied, "I trust you to do the right thing at summer's end." Without hesitation I answered, "Trust me, I will do the right thing."

As it happened, we hired Adam as an intern, and he was magnificent in his job. He was well liked and respected by everybody in the company. As the end of summer approached, my boss came into my office and asked if I had let Adam go. I told him that it would be unethical to dismiss such a talented individual and that he would have to fire me first. Instead, my boss dangled a promotion in front of me as an incentive to do what he asked. I refused, and then resigned. My boss urged me to stay, but I told him it was irrevocable.

In the days and weeks that followed, I realized the import of what I'd done. I had no job, no leads, nowhere to go, and a big mortgage to boot. But despite the fears, I felt almost euphoric! I never lacked for confidence, but for the first time in my life I had something more: I had high self-esteem and a true sense of self-worth. When it came down to values, the worst of bosses had just taught me the best of lessons. By the way, it only took me two weeks to land a better position in another company. I guess my rekindled sense of self-worth came through loud and clear in the interview process.

## Appreciation in Value

In their thought-provoking book *Inner Security and Infinite Wealth*, Stuart Zimmerman and Jared Rosen remind us that many things appreciate in value. A stock appreciates in value, your house appreciates in value. Even your baseball card collection can appreciate in value. You can appreciate in value, too. Your self-worth can skyrocket. When you value yourself and when your actions are aligned with your core value system, your sense of self-worth will increase mightily. But more important, you will live a life of enrichment.

> *If you have integrity, nothing else matters.*
> *If you don't have integrity, nothing else matters.*
> —ALAN SIMPSON

Being fully aware of your core values is the key element in making wise choices in your life. Whether it's buying a house, choosing a partner, or making career decisions, your core values come into play. Your good value system is the starting point and ending point for all the important decisions you will make in your life. Sometimes, however, we can lose sight of our core values or not factor them in enough in our decision-making process.

My friend Bill was being heavily recruited by a large company based in Arizona. Bill's new career opportunity seemed almost too good to be true. As it turned out, it was. Everything seemed in order. A great financial package? Check. A sunny climate? You bet. A great benefits package? Ditto. Exciting products? Once again, check. A boss who had integrity? No.

During the interview process, Bill's potential boss told him several lies including the fib that the company's new product line would roll out earlier than anticipated. Bill already knew from a previous interview that the new products would likely be delayed for more than a year. He also noticed that the company continued to run ads proclaiming that the new products were "coming real soon." The boss also highly inflated the company's sales projections, which were directly tied to Bill's potential bonus package. Although he came away feeling his potential new boss would not necessarily honor his commitments and probably lacked integrity, Bill accepted the job anyway. Maybe he was blinded by the lure of the Arizona sun. You probably guessed the rest of the story. Bill resigned less than a year later when his boss demanded that he run an unethical ad campaign regarding the still-to-be-delivered new products. Bill failed to realize that when your boss lacks the core value of integrity, every other potential benefit is built on quicksand.

## Net Worth Versus Self-Worth

Don't fall into the trap of allowing your net worth to determine your self-worth. How much money you've got stashed away isn't who you are, or even who you can become. Self-worth and net worth are markedly different animals. Author Rick Warren, in his book *The Purpose-Driven Life*, tells us that "our value is not determined by our valuables. The most valuable things in life are not likely to be our things."

During the skyrocketing stock market of the late 1990s, many of us checked our computer screens to see how much money we made that day. If our portfolio was up, we felt great. If it was down, we felt demoralized. That was fine when there were more good days than bad days. But when the market crashed by March of 2000, watching the computer screen on a daily basis was for most an ugly sight. You not only felt demoralized, you felt in a sense devalued as a person. You felt less secure. It's only when you realize that real security resides in those things that could never be taken away that you can continue to feel a high sense of self-worth and self-esteem. Nobody can take away your core values or the essence of your being unless you let them. Don't let them!

> *When our life becomes a true expression of our values we make our greatest contribution to the world.*
> —CHERYL RICHARDSON

When you're a person with good character and good values, you are indeed a person of true wealth. Your real currency is measured not just in money, but the inner security you feel when you are a person of true integrity.

Dawna Markova, in her riveting book *I Will Not Die an Unlived Life*, offers this enlightened perspective on our core values: "Your values are an activating intelligence in your life, guiding you toward the noble tasks that are yours alone to do. There are moments in all our lives that reveal these values. Their significance lies in not only what meaning we make of them, but also what we allow those moments to make of us."

Your solid core values are like a ship arriving in safe harbor, a beacon to which you can always return, especially in stormy weather and today's turbulent times. Remember, when your outside world reflects your inside world, your sense of value and self-worth will literally soar off the charts.

It all boils down to this: We are what we value. As Elvis Presley once said, "Values are like fingerprints. Nobody's are the same, but you leave 'em all over everything you do."

## EXECUTIVE SUMMARY

This chapter hones in on the importance of profitability—but not profit at any cost. Today's business ethics or values are under severe scrutiny. A company's good business ethics adds quality to the overall value of the enterprise.

Likewise, on a personal level, our personal balance sheet has a lot to do with having a good core value system. Our good values enhance our sense of self-equity and self-worth. A good value system is often accompanied by a higher feeling of self-esteem. Our value system allows us a safe harbor to fall back on especially in turbulent times. When you live up to your core values, you are focused and have a clearer sense of purpose. When our outer life is aligned with our inner feelings, we put ourselves in a better position to make a contribution to the world. It all boils down to this; we are in essence that which we value. In the words of Alexander Hamilton, "Those who stand for nothing fall for anything."

### EXERCISE 1: YOUR CORE VALUES

A.  Take another look at your core values listed on pages 144–45. It's important that you narrowcast your values to a manageable number—a number you can get your arms around. Accordingly, try narrowing your core values down to those eight core values that matter most to you. These values should capture the true essence of your authentic self. Remember, nobody can take these core values away from you—unless you let them. These values represent your safe harbor, a place you can always come home to when making life's important decisions.

MY EIGHT MOST IMPORTANT VALUES:

1. _____
2. _____
3. _____
4. _____
5. _____
6. _____
7. _____
8. _____

B.  Is your present job in tune with your core value system? Explain.

_____

_____

_____

C.  Name a time or times in your life when your core values were severely tested. What was the outcome? What did you learn?

_____

_____

_____

D.  Give some examples of how your core values guided you in a positive way in making important decisions in your life.

_____

_____

_____

E.  Have you ever lost sight of your core values in making an important decision in your life?
    If yes, what was the outcome? What did you learn?

    _____

    _____

    _____

F.  What good values did your parents instill in you?

    _____

    _____

    _____

G.  How have your values changed over the years given your life's experiences?

    _____

    _____

    _____

## EXERCISE 2: SELF-WORTH/SELF-ESTEEM

A.  List the times in your life when your sense of self-worth or self-esteem was at its highest.

    _____

    _____

    _____

B.  List the times in your life when your sense of self-worth or self-esteem was at its lowest.
    (What core values did you fall back on to gain or regain your self-worth or self-esteem?)

    _____

    _____

    _____

*Have your core values ever been severely tested?*
*What was the outcome?*
*Do you have a high sense of self-worth?*

# CHAPTER 12

# ESTABLISH TARGETS OF OPPORTUNITY

## Making Your Dreams Come True

*A man is not old until his regrets take the place of his dreams.*
—JOHN BARRYMORE

The final section of the marketing plan defines targets of opportunity, or visions of future products and services that are in keeping with the business you're in. Simply put: A corporation must find opportunities that will allow a company to grow in the future.

In a sense, this is the "dream" section of the Marketing Plan for Life—a place where a company can consider new opportunities after achieving their sales and strategic goals, as set forth in steps one through eleven of this marketing-plan process. However, these targets of opportunity must be consistent with the defined business we should be in, as discussed in point one of the planning process. This ensures that even the most daunting challenge can be realized. A company's core competencies should be used to their fullest extent.

*Never fear the space between your dreams and reality.*
*If you can dream it, you can make it so.*
—BELVA DAVIS

Just like a growing company, your personal targets of opportunity have to do with realizing your dreams. But it's one thing to have dreams, it's another to have pipe dreams. Similar to any good company, you must make sure your dreams are an integral part of who you are. Your dreams should be aligned with your individual core strengths—as well as with your heart.

## Opportunities Galore

There are different types of targets of opportunity that will help enable a company to grow steadily and create incremental business. When this happens, the goals, dreams, and aspirations of both employees and shareholders are often realized. Let's review a few of the ways a company can realize its targets of opportunities for growth.

### New Products and Services

The Walt Disney Company is a great example of layering on new products and services. They started as an animation company, then a movie studio, branched out into theme parks, created a Sunday-night television program. Later, Disney established hundreds of retail stores selling only Disney-branded characters and products. Already an entertainment company, Disney then acquired the ABC network and ESPN as part of their sports entertainment strategy. ESPN, ESPN2, ESPN Classic, ESPN Latin America, and the *ESPN* magazine have since become one of the leading profit centers for the Walt Disney Company.

Layering on new products and services has application on a personal level as well as big business. If you are an author of nonfiction books, you might consider branching out into writing magazine articles, newsletters, a newspaper column, or creating your own Web site. These are all logical extensions that will add to your repertoire of product and service offerings.

## Creating New Divisions

Companies often set up new divisions so they can achieve greater focus in realizing their business goals. Most companies have international divisions that concentrate solely on achieving foreign market penetration. Other companies set up key account divisions because they recognize the proverbial twenty-eighty theory. Namely, 20 percent of your key customers often do 80 percent of the business. Companies also set up "new venture" groups that can focus on bringing incremental business into the company. General Electric set up a financing division that could help people pay for products and services over time. The net result was a big profit center for GE.

We should consider applying the twenty-eighty theory to our personal lives as well. As we talked about earlier in chapter nine, we should strive to divide our time smartly by investing it wisely on that which matters most to us. Wouldn't it be great to spend 80 percent of our time on the important things in our lives?

## Striking Key Alliances and Partnerships

Luxury leather maker Coach collaborated with luxury car maker Lexus to create a Coach Special Edition car. Eddie Bauer collaborated with Ford to create the Eddie Bauer Edition of Ford Explorer. Starbucks and United Airlines forged an alliance to improve in-flight coffee, while extending the Starbucks brand name into overseas markets.

In life as well as business, a complementary and encouraging partner (think marriage or significant other) can make all the difference in the world in realizing your dreams and goals.

Whether you're trying to realize your personal dreams or professional goals, it's absolutely essential that we have positive people (also known as good alliances) around us. Football coach Lou Holtz realized his dreams by doing what he did best, namely coach football—but he also had a positive wife who encouraged him to reach out to make his "impossible dreams" happen. In fact, Lou Holtz had an interesting approach to making his dreams come alive. He'd write his dreams down from one to one hundred in a book and check them off as he achieved them. When he was only an assistant coach at the University of Minnesota, he dared to dream that someday he'd be the head coach of Notre Dame—arguably still the dream job for any college football coach. He also dreamed of winning a national collegiate football championship. He also dreamed he'd visit the White House and eventually meet the pope. Some pretty lofty goals, indeed! But Holtz managed to make his dreams a reality.

Here's how he did it:. He turned around a losing football program as head coach at Minnesota and was eventually awarded the head coaching job at Notre Dame several years later. While at Notre Dame, he won the national championship, which led to meeting the president at the White House, and later met the pope while touring Europe. Holtz wrote his dreams down in a book and checked them off as he made them happen. In a sense, his book of dreams became a book of realities.

*The greatest danger for most of us lies not in setting our aim too high and falling short, but in setting our aim too low and achieving our mark.*
—MICHELANGELO

## Mergers and Acquisitions

Chrysler's acquisition of American Motors years ago is an example of a merger/acquisition with one company trying to reenergize itself with the brand attributes of another. One of Chrysler's main objectives was to acquire AMC's Jeep brand at a time when Chrysler had a less-than-robust image with consumers. It actually worked. Following the acquisition, Chrysler introduced more revolutionary auto designs than any other domestic automotive company, which resulted in tremendous corporate growth.

In chapter two we talked about merging with people who offer complementary capabilities. People who value your strengths and can help you manage around your weaknesses. A healthy marriage, relationship, or encouraging business partner will go a long way in helping you focus and get what you want out of life.

## Creating New Value-Added Streams

The phone companies are highly creative when it comes to creating new value streams, while still staying within the corporate tapestry. When you get your phone bill you are charged extra for these valued services: call waiting, call forwarding, caller ID, call blocking, speed dialing, and call conferencing, just to name a few. Still, other examples of added value streams include the luxury suites at sports stadiums and valet parking at major shopping malls.

We as individuals can also create *value added* by doing what we do best and utilizing our talents to help others. I personally felt valued and gave *value added* by helping my community theater market their annual calendar of local plays. What talents do you offer that can create value for others?

### Licensing

Developing a good licensing program is one of the best ways a company can grow. Licensing should be viewed as a strategic marketing tool to extend the brand into new market categories, while continuing to build brand awareness of the company's core line. While adding new product categories adds to the brand's elasticity, it should also be consistent with the company's brand image and positioning in the marketplace. Ralph Lauren (fashion apparel) moved into top-quality paint. In concert with their licensing partner, Lauren often updated fashion-color palettes on a seasonal basis in the best hardware stores in the country.

In life we often seek to gain skill sets that others possess that will help us make our dreams a reality. We hire skilled architects and creative interior designers to transform our fixer-upper into a dream house. We retain the services of a stockbroker who lends his expertise to help us establish a financial portfolio that will enable us to fulfill our dreams. By passing on part of the dream work to others we can more rapidly realize our own dreams.

Both companies and people are able to realize their targets of opportunity (and in a sense, their dreams) by having the courage to create an extended self, while not losing sight of who they are. They create new opportunities for growth but still stay within the parameters of their very core competency. They know how far they can reach to make their targets of opportunity a reality.

One word of caution here: Don't reach for something that is unattainable. I might dream of becoming the chief marketing executive for my favorite major league baseball team, but if my goal was to become the chief financial officer, my dream of joining my beloved team would turn out to be a nightmare. Without the necessary skills and interests for the job, I'd be going to my weakness, not my strength. Dream big—but in your dreams don't lose sight of who you are.

## The Impossible Dream

U.S. Olympic hockey coach Herb Brooks had a dream that he could guide a bunch of young amateurs to a gold medal in the 1980 Winter Olympics at Lake Placid, New York. His goal was labeled the "impossible dream," considering his team stood no chance against the experienced, professional Soviet team, who at the time literally dominated international hockey. In fact, the Soviets demolished the American squad of college kids 10–3 in an exhibition game at New York's Madison Square Garden just one week before the Olympics.

But Coach Brooks convinced his young, inexperienced squad to buy into the impossible dream. In what is now referred to as the "miracle on ice," the Americans stunned the world by upsetting the heavily favored Russian team 4–3. To this day, no single upset in sports history is more fondly remembered in the United States. As the final seconds of the game ticked away, announcer Al Michaels made his now famous call: "Do you believe in miracles? Yes!" The American team went on to secure the gold medal and the hearts of all Americans by beating Finland several days later. Coach Brooks encouraged and motivated his players to believe in their dreams. By doing so, his dreams became their reality. It also became a legendary sports story for the ages.

> *It all started with a dream and a mouse.*
>
> —WALT DISNEY

Walt Disney tells his own story about his dreams. His boyhood dream was to draw comic strips. But as a young man he was strongly advised by a Kansas City editor to give up drawing because he lacked artistic flair and talent. Disney kept knocking on doors, but he was continually rejected. Finally, a church hired Disney to draw some basic publicity material. While working out of an old dingy garage, Disney befriended a small mouse. Disney's new little rodent friend inspired him to create the character of Mickey Mouse. Before long, both Disney and the mouse became part of bigger dreams. You know the rest of the story.

> *Move into your castle in the sky as if it were your right to do so.*
>
> —GENE LUNDRUM

Dreams certainly did come true for Oprah Winfrey, but only after trials, tribulations, and just plain hard work. Oprah was born in humble surroundings in a small farming community in Mississippi. As a child she was sexually abused and moved to Nashville, Tennessee, to live with her father. As a youngster, Oprah read a lot of books about heroes and heroines that inspired her to have dreams of her own. After attending Tennessee State University, she began working in a Nashville radio and television station. Later, Oprah moved to Baltimore where she hosted a TV chat show called *People are Talking*. The show became a hit and she was asked to host another talk show—A.M. Chicago. Her major competition in this time slot was Phil Donahue, who at the time, literally owned the daytime talk show market. After just a few months, Winfrey's unique, warm, and empathetic personality had won her considerably more viewers than Donahue. Oprah vaulted to first in the TV ratings. Her success catapulted her to national acclaim and a role in Steven Spielberg's 1985 film *The Color Purple*, for which she was nominated for an Oscar for "best supporting actress."

Winfrey then launched the Oprah Winfrey Show in 1986. It became a nationally syndicated program. The show remained the number-one talk show for sixteen consecutive seasons—earning thirty-five Emmy Awards at the time of this writing. Her show became the highest-rated talk show in television history. As her ratings increased, Oprah's subject matter gradually shifted from sensational topics to topics that provided possibilities for people to transform their lives. She also began an on-air book club designed to get the country more interested in reading—especially about inspirational subject matter.

From humble beginnings, Oprah has established herself as a person who not only envisions but enlightens and encourages millions of people around the world to believe that their dreams can also come true. If she did it, so can you.

Following and achieving your dream is not a direct highway. Like any other of life's challenges, there will be potholes and boulders strewn across the road. Once you've defined your dream, go for it. Go for it with all the gusto and positive energy you can muster. The key is to have the courage to keep going. Keep heading in the direction of your dreams and you will make them a reality. The point is: If you can dream it—if you can visualize it—you can do it. As Eleanor Roosevelt said, "The future belongs to those who believe in the beauty of their dreams."

What are your dreams? Can you visualize them? Have you always wanted to write a screenplay or a book? Do you dream of starting your own company with a trusted partner? Do you dream of spending more quality time with your family? Do you dream of setting up a charitable foundation? Do you dream of sailing around the world? Do you dream of a blissful retirement? Do you dream of being a person who can pull the ripcord and take action on the important things in your life? We all have the power within our indomitable human spirit to make our dreams a reality. If you build your dreams from the heart and pursue them with passion, you can accomplish anything you set out to do. But let me make this abundantly clear: We all need to have a dream. We need to allow our dreams to fly and fly high. Don't put your dreams on a short string. Dream on. Set your dreams free. The real tragedy of life would be not to have a dream at all.

*Believe in the power of your dreams even if no one else does, because when you make your dreams a reality, it won't matter who doubted you.*

**—JOSH HINDS**

## Don't Let Anyone Attack Your Dreams

It's just a fact of life. There is always going to be someone out there who will try to steal or hinder your dreams. Don't abdicate your dreams for others who raise their eyebrows. Don't give in to doubting Thomases. There will always be pundits and naysayers who sneer at you and try to discourage you by planting the seeds of doubt. We can't give in to these people. We're not puppets on their proverbial string.

Author and national speaker Larry Hinds tells us that there's always a "thief" that goes around trying to steal our dreams. They try to rob or alter our mental state needed to obtain our goals. These thieves often disguise themselves in different forms. Sometimes it's a discouraging parent, or a doubting partner or coworker. Sometimes the thief comes from a friend who doesn't believe you can accomplish your dreams and just doesn't want you to get hurt by trying.

Don't let other people attack your dreams. Here are just a few examples as to why we should not always listen to our doubters:

- When Steve Jobs of Apple went to Hewlett-Packard to get them interested in his and Steve Wozniak's personal computer, he was turned down summarily because he had not finished college yet.

- Very few so-called marketing experts thought Evian could sell still water for more than two dollars a bottle. After all, who would pay for water that already comes out of a tap?

- Barbra Streisand's mother told her she wasn't pretty enough to be an actress and that she wasn't a good enough singer to be a star.

- A New York publisher actually told James Michener that he should stick to editing and not try to be a writer. Undaunted, Michener wrote his first book, *Tales of the South Pacific,* which won him the Pulitzer Prize for literature!

- As a young man, Leonard Bernstein was constantly harassed by his father to give up his music and go out and get a real job. Years later, after Bernstein went on to become one of America's most successful composers, his dad was asked why he didn't do more to encourage his son. To which his father replied, "Well, how was I supposed to know that he'd grow up to be 'the' Leonard Bernstein?"

Oliver Wendell Holmes summed it up best when he said, "Many people die with their music still in them." The real tragedy is when we ourselves allow our dreams to be stolen from us. Stand up for your dreams!

## Does Your Personality Fit Your Dreams?

Martha Beck, in her delightful book *Finding Your Own North Star,* tells us about the types of personality profiles that bode well or ill for making your dreams a reality. Here's my brief synopsis of each personality:

### Chaos Commando

This is a person whose dreams are constantly changing. They come up with a new dream until they get bored again. The net result: a lot of scurrying around and dabbling with very few dreams being fulfilled.

### Big Dreamer/Little Doer

You know this person. This is the dreamer type that loves sitting in their office planning their illustrious career. On the surface, they seemingly do all the right stuff. They practice creative visualization, do daily affirmations, and write detailed mission statements. They read all the good self-help and motivational books they can find. But in the end—they do nothing. They take no action. The truth is this person is more comfortable in their imagination than they are in the real world. Unless this person learns to take pragmatic action, their dreams will never become a reality.

### Rock of Gibraltar

This is the steady-as-a-rock type. They meticulously complete every assignment and every mundane aspect of their job. But don't ask this person to do anything but forge straight ahead like a bull in a China closet. Although they get their job done, don't ask them to think outside the box. Don't ask them to come up with new responses or creative solutions.

### Realist

This is that wonderful person that keeps track of all the details. This person is great at arranging schedules and following up to ensure that every assignment gets meticulously done. This is a person that falls in love with other people's visions. In a sense they live vicariously through others—by helping make other people's dreams a reality.

### Dream Maker

I would personally like to add another type of person to the profile list and that's the Dream Maker. The Dream Maker not only has the vision but they also know how to make things happen. They clearly understand that by accenting the positive aspects of each profile, they'll end up with a team that has complementary capabilities to accomplish wonderful things. The Dream Maker readily understands that the person who can read the road map might not be the best driver. Dream Makers have vision. They can think outside the box, but they also have enough focus and "tunnel vision" to know how to cross the goal line. They know how to take people with different personality profiles to all pull the oar in the same direction and sing off the same sheet of music. Dream Makers do much more than dream about building castles in the sky. They actually lay the foundation and orchestrate the building of the castle, brick by glorious brick.

Ask yourself these questions: Which one of the profiles we discussed describes you best? Are you a combination of several profiles? Do you surround yourself with people of complementary capabilities that will allow you to make your dreams a reality? Answering these questions honestly will help you manage your efforts properly to realize your dreams.

> *If I can dream, I can act. And if I can act, I can become.*
> —POH YU KHING

## Having the Courage to Fulfill Your Dreams

People who fulfill their dreams have at least one thing in common: They have the courage to act to make their dreams come true. Courage is the lynchpin that will allow you to achieve your dreams. If you don't exhibit courage, you'll never want it bad enough to keep going when things look their bleakest. It's been said, if you don't make your dreams happen, you may not have the courage necessary to ever dream again. According to author Peter McWilliams, we must be willing to pay the price for achieving our dreams. We must be willing to come out of our comfort zone. McWilliams says, "We must be willing to be uncomfortable. Lack of comfort, however, is a small price to pay for actualizing your dreams."

The inspiring story of young Wimbledon tennis champion Maria Sharapova reminds us that the American dream is still alive and kicking even if you happened to be born in Siberia. When Maria was a baby, her family moved to escape the Chernobyl nuclear fallout. The Sharapovas wanted a better way of life for their daughter so they decided to uproot the family and move to the United States with only seven hundred dollars in their pocket. The parent's dream was that their daughter Maria would be accepted and excel in Nick Bolletieri's famed tennis academy in Florida for youngsters who showed tennis potential at an early age.

On the day the Sharapovas were leaving Russia, Maria's grandmother observed her seven-year old granddaughter calmly packing and carefully folding her clothes as if "she was preparing for her destiny." Destiny arrived earlier than expected for Maria. At the young age of seventeen, she shocked the tennis world by upsetting the heavily favored Serena Williams to win the 2004 Wimbledon Tennis Championship. Maria and her family proved that dreams do come true, but it takes courage and the right risk to turn dreams into reality.

Erma Bombeck puts having courage and having dreams in perspective: "There are people who put their dreams in a little box and say yes, I've got dreams, of course I've got dreams. Then they put the box away and bring it out once in a while to look at it and say, yeah, they're still there. These are great dreams but they never get out of the box. It takes an uncommon amount of guts to put your dreams on the line, to hold them up and say, how good or bad am I? That's where courage comes in."

*The poor man is not he who is without a cent, but he who is without a dream.*
—HARRY KEMP

One of my all-time favorite movies is *Field of Dreams,* starring Kevin Costner. As a kid, I, too, dreamed of becoming a Major League Baseball player and playing with the greats of the game. In my favorite scene, John Kinsella and doctor Moonlight Graham (convincingly played by an aging Burt Lancaster) have a riveting discussion about a man's dreams. Let me break down the scene for you: Kinsella asks Graham what it was like to play in only one major league game. Graham responded by saying he never even hit the ball out of the infield. The game ended and the season was over. Then the aging Graham responded reflectively, "Back then I thought there'll be other days—I didn't realize that that was the only day."

When it comes to your dreams, don't harbor any regrets that you didn't go for it full-bore. If you do, you'll regret it not only now but later. As Mark Twain tells us, "Twenty years from now you'll be more disappointed by the things you did not do than the ones you did do. So throw away the bowlines. Sail away from safe harbor. Catch trade winds in your sails. Explore. Dream. Discover."

President John F. Kennedy built the new frontier and his dreams of a better America while being inspired by one of his favorite quotes from George Bernard Shaw: "Some people look at the world as it is and ask why. I dream of worlds that never were and ask why not."

Reach out to touch the stars. Have the courage and fortitude to make your dreams a reality. Don't be afraid to stray from the shoreline. But most of all, harbor no regrets.

I'd like to close this final chapter with this exhilarating quote from John Barrymore: "A man is not old until his regrets take the place of his dreams."

## EXECUTIVE SUMMARY

The final chapter defines the various targets of opportunity or visions of future products and services that will allow a company to grow in the future. In essence, this is the "dream section" of the marketing-plan process.

On a personal level, each of us has our own dreams. It's up to us to make our dreams a reality. There will always be doubters who will try to discourage us from fulfilling our dreams. We have to have the courage and commitment to make our dreams happen. We can't lock up our dreams in a safe-deposit box. They must be free to fly high.

But most of all, when it comes to our dreams we should harbor no regrets. If we can dream it, we can do it. Remember the haunting words of John Barrymore: "A man is not old until his regrets take the place of his dreams."

## EXERCISE 1: WRITING DOWN YOUR DREAMS

Write down your top five personal dreams that you would like to make a reality. For now, don't worry about prioritizing each dream—just let it flow. Even your wildest dreams count. Remember, we eventually all run out of time. What we can never do is run out of dreams.

1. _____
   _____

2. _____
   _____

3. _____
   _____

4. _____
   _____

5. _____
   _____

## EXERCISE 2: REALIZING YOUR DREAMS

Give two examples in your life when you reached out to make your dreams a reality.

1. _____
   _____

2. _____
   _____

## EXERCISE 3: UNFULFILLED DREAM

Do you presently harbor any regrets for not going all out to fulfill an important dream in your life? If so, please explain.

_____

_____

_____

_____

## EXERCISE 4: DREAM INSPIRATION

Take the time to jot down a movie, play, book, song, piece of art, or sporting event that inspired or inspires you most to realize your dreams.

A.  Movie (for example, *Field of Dreams*)

_____

_____

B.  Play (for example, *Man of La Mancha*)

_____

_____

C.  Song (for example, "One Moment in Time")

_____

_____

_____

D.  Piece of Art (for example, Michelangelo's *David*)

_____

_____

_____

E.  Sporting Event (for example, the Miracle on Ice)

_____

_____

_____

F.  Historical Event (for example, Churchill's courage to fight the tyranny of Hitler)

_____

_____

_____

Keep these elements of inspiration in a visible place, and revisit them often as a constant reminder to act on your dreams.

*Do you have great dreams that you have put on hold? Are you chasing your own dream or are you living vicariously through the dreams of others?*

# Epilogue

*"Life should not be a journey to the grave with the intention of arriving safely in a pretty and well-preserved body, but rather to skid broadside in a cloud of smoke, thoroughly used up, totally worn out, and loudly proclaiming 'Wow! What a ride!' "*
**—ATTRIBUTED TO HUNTER S. THOMPSON**

An illuminating thing happened to me while writing this book. On my way to trying to help you discover what really mattered most, I had a personal epiphany. I discovered myself. I also discovered I was, in essence, living a white lie. The very things I was encouraging you to do were the things I needed to do for myself. It never dawned on me that my own book would go a long way in altering my own life, for the better.

In the introduction of this book, I underscored that I was not just coming along for the ride, but that I was going to take the same Marketing Plan for Life journey as you, the reader. I never imagined at the time that I would be taking what amounted to be the most exhilarating trip of my life. Almost eerily, each chapter as I was writing it, seemed to mirror precisely what was going on in my personal life at that exact moment in time.

For instance, when I was urging you to discover your true calling or purpose, my own purpose seemed to come into sharper focus. I suddenly had a much clearer picture as to where I was going in my life and why. On my way to exhorting you to become your genuine or authentic self, I realized that I wasn't the person I always wanted to become.

When I was encouraging you to invest your time wisely and take action on those things that mattered most, I recognized that I was virtually paralyzed when it came time to take action on things that mattered most to me. It hadn't really occurred to me that many of the important things in my life were put on hold for the sake of a bigger marketing challenge—or for that matter, a fatter paycheck.

As I was extolling you to consider reinventing yourself, I hadn't realized I was in the very process of redefining myself and the direction I would take in my own life.

I was always concerned about my legacy, but now I know it most likely lies somewhere in encouraging and motivating others—perhaps, somewhere within the very pages of this book. Additionally, I confirmed that the very process I used to make money could now be turned up to a higher level—to also make meaning.

So, armed with my own Marketing Plan for Life process echoing in my ear, I pulled my own personal ripcord and took the following action on my own life/work plan:

■ I courageously (for me) resigned from my lucrative post as a corporate senior vice president of marketing because the job was no longer totally aligned with my life's purpose and the need to more clearly define my legacy.

■ I started a new company called ThirdWind. The new company will be dedicated to helping corporations and individuals discover what truly matters most to them. ThirdWind will not only offer a series of worldwide Marketing Plan for Life seminars but will also offer a plethora of other products and services as well. These will include audio and videotapes, a Web site newsletter and a unique daily planner book called "LifeTimer," which allows you to balance on a daily basis both your work and your personal life. Additionally, both radio and TV programming focusing on the subject matter of this book is currently under development.

■ Taking care to not throw the baby out with the bathwater, we also reinstituted our marketing consulting firm called BrandMark, which has several major clients. BrandMark will help us stay financially grounded as we grow our new ThirdWind company business.

■ However, my own personal journey would not be complete without making one more important move—the move of my boyhood dreams—the move to the Big Sur coast near stunningly beautiful Carmel-by-the-Sea, California. It's a place where fresh air still matters—a place where twinkling stars dance above a white-capped majestic sea. What more appropriate place to locate the headquarters of our new ThirdWind Company? No more waiting for the perfect moment that never seems to come. This time, I'm really moving and taking the leap to the land of my dreams.

In closing, I hope this book serves as a catalyst to start you on your own personal journey. A journey of rediscovery, a journey that helps you define your true purpose. A journey that will remind you to invest your time on those things that matter most. Remember, as you embark on your journey, the wonderful words of Ursula K. Le Guin: "It is good to have an end to journey toward; but it is the journey that matters, in the end."

# Let Us Hear from You

Now that you've read the book and completed your workshop exercises, you have all the tools you need to put your Marketing Plan for Life into action.

You're on an exciting journey. I hope this plan has the same positive impact on your life as it did on mine and others in our workshop seminars. Let me hear from you by e-mail at rmf@marketingplanforlife.com.

# Index

Page numbers in **bold** indicate exercises or tables; those in *italic* indicate illustrations.

Abraham, Daniel, 45
Achieving your sales goals. *See* Sales goals, achieving your
Acquisitions as opportunities, 158
Action
  advertising element, 94, **108, 109**
  physical closeness to action for distribution planning, 113–14
  strategy and, 39–40, 41–44, 47–48, **48–49**
Advertising campaign, building, *xiii,* 93–109
  action (buy in) element of, 94, **108, 109**
  age and diminishing creativity, 97
  back-of-mind vs. top-of-mind awareness, 97
  buy in (take action) element of, 94, **108, 109**
  chat rooms and word of mouth advertising, 96
  childlike creativity, 97, 106, **107**
  classic ad campaigns, 95–96
  constructive criticism, 105
  creative impact element of, 94, 98–100, 101–4, 106, **107–9**
  creative visualization, 105, 129
  criticism, handling, 104–5, 107, **108**
  environment for creativity, 103–4, 107, 113

executive summary, 106–7
exercises, **107–9**
failure, fear of, 98, 106, **108**
feedback element of, 94
finishing projects and, 99
frequency element of, 94
handling criticism, 104–5, 107, **108**
ideas for creativity, 101–2, 103, **108**
importance of, 93–95, 106
left brain (logical)/right brain (creative), 97–98, **98,** 106, **107**
perfection and creativity, 98, 106, **108**
presentation dynamics element of, 94, 100–101
process, creativity as a, 101–2, 106
reach element of, 94
reawakening your creative spirit, 100
reflection on, 109
right brain (creative)/left brain (logical), 97–98, **98,** 106, **107**
rituals for creativity, 102–3
share of mind vs. share of market, 97
top-of-mind vs. back-of-mind awareness, 97
vision element of, 94, 105, **109**
"whispering campaign," 96
word of mouth, 96

workspace (personal) for creativity, 104
  *See also* Distribution, planning your
Affirmations for goals, 127
Aging
  creativity, diminishing with age, 97
  values and, 146–47, **147**
Alexander the Great, 33
Alka-Seltzer, 95
Alliances as opportunities, 157–58
Allston, John, 81, 85
*A.M. Chicago,* 160
Amazon.com, 105
American Motors, 158
Anheuser-Busch, 16
Apple Computer, 39, 55, 71–72, 74, 76, 89, 97, 162
Appreciation in value, 149
Aronson, Eric, xi
Arthur Anderson, 141
*Artist's Way, The* (Cameron), 98
Assessing the market. *See* Market assessment
Authentic Collection (Majestic Athletic), 29
Authenticity, 29–30, 32, 35–36, **37–38.** *See also* Target customer, identifying
Avis, 40

Avoiding your strengths, 19
Awareness, top-of-mind vs. back-of-mind, 97
Azdak, Roy, 104

Back-of-mind vs. top-of-mind awareness, 97
Backward, living our lives, 34–35
Baker, Dan, 34, 64, 115, 144, 147
Balance between work/life, 9
Balance sheet. *See* Profit and loss analysis
Balancing your personal integrity account, 147–48, 151
Baldwin, Faith, 56
Ball, Bill, 72
Balzac, Honoré de, 8
Barrymore, John, 155, 166
Bauer, Eddie, 29
Beane, Billy, 15
Beck, Martha, 163
Beethoven, Ludwig van, 21, 131
Beetle (Volkswagen), 97
Being true to yourself, 30
Benefits/features (communication key), 70, 71, **79**
Ben & Jerry's, 77, 86
Bennett, Tony, 57
Berkshire Hathaway, 143–44
Bernbach, William, 95
Bernstein, Leonard, 162
Berry, Jon, 34
Berthiaume, André, 36
Bezos, Jeff, 105
Big, thinking, 131–32
Big Dreamer/Little Doer personality profile, 163
BMW Group's Mini Cooper, 95–96
Bodhidharma, 41
Bombeck, Erma, 165
Boomer generation and values, 146–47
Brand building, personal, 70–71, 72–74, 78, **79, 80.** *See also* Communication keys, hitting your
*Brand Called You, The* (Montoya and Vandehey), 73
BrandMark, 172
Brecht, Bertolt, 58
Bronson, Po, 5, 6, 89
Brooklyn Bridge, 128

Brooks, Herb, 159–60
Brown, H. Jackson, 115
Brown, Less, 43–44
Browning, Robert, 131
Buckingham, Marcus, 17
Bud Light (Budweiser), 16
Budweiser, 15–16, 114
Buffett, Warren, 43, 143
Building a high-impact advertising campaign. *See* Advertising campaign, building
Building on your key strengths, 15–16
Building your personal brand. *See* Communication keys, hitting your
Burger King, 40, 96
Bushnell, Nolan, 42
Business creation of a legacy, 83–84, 89–90
Business you're in, defining, *xiii*, 1–11
    balance between work/life, 9
    constant redefinition, 2–4
    core competency, staying with, 3, 4, 56
    executive summary, 9
    exercises, **10–11**
    importance of, 1–2, 9
    life of purpose, 5–8, **7, 9, 10**
    obsession vs. passion, 9
    passions, igniting your, 4, **7,** 8–9, **11**
    purpose, defining, 4–8, **7, 9, 10**
    redefinition, constant, 2–4
    reflection on, 11
    self-discovery questions, **10–11**
    "true north" (purpose), defining, 4–8, **7, 9, 10**
    unfinished business and defining purpose in life, 4
    unhappiness, defined, 9
    *See also* Market assessment
Buy in (take action) element of advertising, 94, **108, 109**
Byrne, Robert, 1, 5, 9

Cabbage Patch Kids, 70
Calculated risks, 44
Call to action, 39–40, 41–44, 47–48, **48–49**
Cameron, Julia, 98, 99
Campbell Soup, 96

Capitalizing on your strengths. *See* Market assessment
Capra, Frank, 100
Capriati, Jennifer, 59
Career/professional goals, **135**
Careers, defining ourselves by, xii–xiii, 118
Carlin, George, 31
Carnegie, Andrew, 42
Casals, Pablo, 69
Catalina Channel, 120
"Cause marketing," business legacy, 84
Chadwick, Florence, 120
Chaos Commando personality profile, 163
Charitable contributions
    business legacy, 83, 90
    personal legacy, 86–87, 90, **91**
Charmin, 95
Chat rooms and word of mouth advertising, 96
Chico's, 72–73, 113
Children
    creativity of, 97, 106, **107**
    personal legacy of, 84–85, 90, **91**
Choices, authentic, 35
*Chronos* (linear) time, 114
Chrysler, 158
Churchill, Winston, 4, 120
Citibank, 148
Cities' reinvention of themselves, 55
Classic ad campaigns, 95–96
Classic Coke (Coca-Cola), 31
Clemmer, Jim, 140
Clifton, Donald, 17
Clinton, Hillary, 57
Coach, 54–55, 157
Coca-Cola, 30–31, 96
*Color Purple, The,* 161
Communication keys, hitting your, *xiii,* 69–80
    brand building, personal, 70–71, 72–74, 78, **79, 80**
    consistency for, 72
    difference, making a, 77–78, **80**
    differentiation benefit of specialization, 73
    executive summary, 78
    exercises, **79–80**
    expertise (presumed) benefit of specialization, 73

features/benefits (key), 70, 71, **79**
importance of, 69–70, 78
making a difference, 77–78, **80**
marketing uniqueness (key), 70, 71, 74–76, 78
multidimensional world and uniqueness, 75
name (key), 70, 71, **79**
narrowcasting, 73–74, **79**
perceived value of specialization, 73
perception (positive) importance, 71, 72–73
personal brand building, 70–71, 72–74, 78, **79, 80**
presumed expertise benefit of specialization, 73
product/service (key), 70, 71, **79**
reflection on, 80
respecting your uniqueness, 76
specialization, 73–74, **79**
strength focus benefit of specialization, 73
trust, building, 72–73
understandability benefit of specialization, 73
uniqueness of marketing (key), 70, 71, 74–76, 78
value (perceived) of specialization, 73
*See also* Reach, expanding your
Community programs
business legacy, 83, 90
personal legacy, 86–87
Companies' reinvention of themselves, 54–56
Competition analysis, 15, 16
Complementary capabilities, 18, 20, 158
Consistency for brand, 72
Constant redefinition, 2–4
Constructive criticism, 105
Core competency, staying with, 3, 4, 56
Core values, identifying, 144–46, **144–46,** 148, 149, 150, 151, **151–53**
Corporate failures, 139–40, 141
Costner, Kevin, 57, 165
Courage
dreams, fulfilling, 164–65, 166
risk-taking and, 47, 48
Creating a legacy. *See* Reach, expanding your

Creative impact element of advertising, 94, 98–100, 101–4, 106, **107–9.** *See also* Advertising campaign, building
Creative (right brain)/logical (left brain), 97–98, **98,** 106, **107**
Creative visualization, 105, 129
Credit Suisse First Boston, 143
Crispin Porter + Boguksy, 96
Criticism, handling, 104–5, 107, **108**
Cronkite, Walter, 72
Cycles, weathering, *xiii,* 53–67
cities' reinvention of themselves, 55
companies' reinvention of themselves, 54–56
core competency, staying with, 3, 4, 56
dedication and adventure (first Wind of Life), 58
defining moments of life, 59–64, **65–66**
discovery (third Wind of Life), 58–59
executive summary, 64
exercises, **65–67**
importance of, 53–54, 64
layering-on concept, 53, 54, 55–56, 64
life cycles, 54, 64
logos, redesigning, 54–55
making your mark (second Wind of Life), 58
passages in life, 58–59
past, importance for perspective on future, 64, **66–67**
personal reinvention, 56–58, 64, **67**
product layering-on concept, 53, 54, 55–56, 64
reflection on, 67
reinventing yourself, 56–58, 64, **67**
Winds of Life, 58–59
*See also* Communication keys, hitting your

Daily affirmations for goals, 127
Daily planner book (LifeTimer), 172
*Dances with Wolves,* 57
*Dash* (Aronson), xi
Davis, Belva, 156
Davis, Jeffrey, 120
Deangeles, Barbara, 76

Dedication and adventure (first Wind of Life), 58
Defining
legacy (your), **90**
moments of life, 59–64, **65–66**
ourselves by our careers, xii–xiii, 118
Defining business you're in. *See* Business you're in, defining
Demographics for target customer, 27–28, 36
Depression-era and values, 146
DeVito, Danny, 56
Difference, making a, 77–78, **80**
Differentiation benefit of specialization, 73
Disbennett-Lee, Rachelle, 22–23
Discomfort, leading to action, 43–44
Discovering authentic you. *See* Target customer, identifying
*Discovering Your North Star* (Reighard), 30, 59
Discovery (third Wind of Life), 58–59
Disney, Roy, 146
Disney, Walt, 131, 160
Disraeli, Benjamin, 41
Distribution, planning your, *xiii,* 111–24
action, physical closeness to, 113–14
*chronos* (linear) time, 114
distributing time wisely, **121**
environment, supportive, 103–4, 107, 113
equalizer, time as, 115
executive summary, 120
exercises, *121,* 121–22, **122–24**
fleeting quality of time, 119–20
gift of time, 115, 118
heartbeats in a lifetime, 119
importance of, 111–12, 120
investing vs. spending time, 115, 116–18, *117, 121,* 121–22, **122–24**
*kairos* (quality) time, 114
location for, 113–14, 120
negative energy, avoiding, 113
positive energy, power of, 112–13
quality time with quality people, 112–13, 114, 115, 119, 120
real life, getting a, 118–19
reflection on, 124
spending time wisely, 115–16, 157

Distribution (*cont.*)
terminal illness, thinking of life as, 118
time, distributing wisely, **121**
"time off," gift of, 119
timing for, 114
vacations, gift of, 119
*See also* Sales goals, achieving your
Divisions (new) as opportunities, 157
Dockers (Levi Strauss), 13–14
Dole, Bob, 77
Donahue, Phil, 160
Doubters of dreams, 162–63, 166
Dream Maker personality profile, 164
Dreams, **166–69.** *See also* Opportunity targets, establishing
Duke University, 8

Easterlin, Richard, 34
"Easterlin Paradox," 34
Eddie Bauer, xiii, 29, 157
Edison, Thomas, 131
Einstein, Albert, 97, 131
Eisenhower, Dwight D., 57, 141
Eliot, George, 27
Email for Marketing Plan for Life, 175
Emerson, Ralph Waldo, xi, xii, 21, 22, 82, 87
*Empire Strikes Back, The,* 41
*English Roses, The* (Madonna), 57
Enoughness concept, 34
Enrichment (personal), 33–35
Enron, 139, 141
Environment, supportive, 103–4, 107, 113
Equalizer, time as, 115
Eskew, Mike, 3
Establishing targets of opportunity. *See* Opportunity targets, establishing
Evaluating strengths and weaknesses, 13, 14–15, 16–17, **23–24**
Event marketing, business legacy, 83
Eveready's Energizer Bunny, 95
Everyday good deeds, personal legacy, 88, 90, **92**
Evian, 162
Executive summaries
advertising campaign, building, 106–7
business you're in, defining, 9

communication keys, hitting your, 78
cycles, weathering, 64
distribution, planning your, 120
market assessment, 23
opportunity targets, establishing, 165
profit and loss analysis, 151
reach, expanding your, 89–90
sales goals, achieving your, 133
strategy, launching your, 47–48
Exercises
advertising campaign, building, **107–9**
business you're in, defining, **10–11**
communication keys, hitting your, **79–80**
cycles, weathering, **65–67**
distribution, planning your, *121,* 121–22, **122–24**
market assessment, **23–26**
opportunity targets, establishing, **166–69**
profit and loss analysis, **151–53**
reach, expanding your, **90–92**
sales goals, achieving your, **134–38**
strategy, launching your, **48–52**
target customer, identifying, **37–38**
Expanding your reach. *See* Reach, expanding your
Expertise (presumed) benefit of specialization, 73

Failure, fear of
advertising campaign, building, 98, 106, **108**
sales goals, achieving your, 132, 133, **138**
Family goals, **134**
*Fast Company,* 33, 35
Fear of committing to action, 45. *See also* Failure, fear of
Feather, William, 18
Features/benefits (communication key), 70, 71, **79**
FedEx, 131–32
Feedback element of advertising, 94
*Field of Dreams,* 85, 165–66
Figuring out who you are, who you want to become. *See* Business you're in, defining

Financial goals, **135–36**
*Finding Your Own North Star* (Beck), 163
Finishing projects, 99
First Wind of Life (dedication and adventure), 58
Fleeting quality of time, 119–20
Focusing on goals, 127
*Forbes,* 142
Ford, 28, 157
Forming your value system, 146–47, **147**
Foster, Jodie, 112
Frankl, Victor, 63
Free the Children, 77–78
Frequency element of advertising, 94
Fulfillment from legacy, 82

Gandhi, Mohandas, 4, 82
Garry, Maryanne, 64
Gauguin, Paul, 104–5
Gaulle, Charles de, 42
General Electric (GE), 156
Gibbs, Joe, 57
Gide, André, 33
Gift of time, 115, 118
Giving back for legacy, 82, 83–84, 86–87, 90, **91**
Glenn, John, 56
Goals vs. objectives, 126–27. *See also* Sales goals, achieving your
Goethe, Johann Wolfgang von, 17, 111
Gogh, Vincent van, 99
Good deeds (everyday), personal legacy, 88, 90, **92**
Grant, Ulysses, 128
*Great Bridge, The* (McCullough), 128
Greatness, going for, 22–23, **25**
Green Bay Packers, 17
Growth goals (personal), **136–37**

Hamilton, Alexander, 139, 151
*Hamlet* (Shakespeare), 35, 36
Handling criticism, 104–5, 107, **108**
Happiness, 33–35
Harley-Davidson, 39, 97
Havner, Vance, 39
Hawthorne, Nathaniel, 32
Health goals, **134–35**

Heartbeats in a lifetime, 119
Heraclitus, 56
Hertz, 40
Hewlett-Packard, 162
Higher meaning, searching for, 88–89, 90
Hillary, Sir Edmund, 28
Hinds, Josh, 161, 162
Hinds, Larry, 162
Hitting your communication keys. *See* Communication keys, hitting your
Hoffman, Hans, 31
Hole in the Wall Gang Camp, 87
Holmes, Oliver Wendell, 2, 163
Holtz, Lou, 157–58
Honda, 97
Honesty for authenticity, 36
Hope, Bob, 72
Hugo, Victor, 101
Hypocrisy, avoiding, 32, 36
Hyundai, 97

Iacocca, Lee, 28, 115
IBM, 97
Ideas for creativity, 101–2, 103, **108**
Identifying core values, 144–46, **144–46,** 148, 149, 150, 151
Identity card (new), 17, **26**
Impossible dreams, 159–61
Improving lives of others by legacy, 82, 83–84, 85
Inaction, society plagued with, 42
"Influentials," 34
*Influentials: One American in Ten Tells the Other Nine, How to Vote, Where to Eat, and What to Buy, The* (Keller and Berry), 34
*Inner Security and Infinite Wealth* (Zimmerman and Rosen), 149
Integrity account (personal), balancing, 147–48, 151
Investing vs. spending time, 115, 116–18, *117, 121,* 121–22, **122–24**
iPod (Apple Computer), 55
*It's a Wonderful Life,* 88
*I Will Not Die an Unlived Life* (Markova), 4, 150

Jackie Robinson Foundation, 87
Jacob, Stefan, 77
Jobs, Steve, 89, 162
Johnson, Earvin ("Magic"), 72
Johnson & Johnson (J&J), 142–43

*Kairos* (quality) time, 114
Keller, Ed, 34
Keller, Helen, 21
Kemp, Harry, 165
Kennedy, John F., 165
Kersey, Cynthia, 6, 129, 132
Khing, Poh Yu, 164
Kielburger, Craig, 77–78
Kierkegaard, Soren, 53, 64
*Kindergarten Cop,* 56
King, Martin Luther, Jr., 72, 131
Klein, Calvin, 1
Kohlberg, Jerome, Jr., 141
Kohlberg, Kravis, Roberts and Company, 141
Kozlowski, Dennis, 140
Krzyzewski, Mike (Coach "K"), 8

Lancaster, Burt, 165
Lao-tzu, 13, 16
Las Vegas, 55
Launching your strategy. *See* Strategy, launching your
Laura Ashley, xiii, 129
Lay, Kenneth L., 139
Layering-on concept, 53, 54, 55–56, 64
Left brain (logical)/right brain (creative), 97–98, **98,** 106, **107**
Legacy, creating. *See* Reach, expanding your
Le Guin, Ursula K., 173
Leisure time and travel goals, **137**
Leonardo da Vinci, 99
Less is more, 31, **38**
Levi Strauss, 13–14, 14–15
Lexus, 157
Licensing as opportunities, 159
Life cycles, 54, 64
*Life Matters* (Merrill and Merrill), 114
Life of purpose, 5–8, **7,** 9, **10**
LifeTimer (daily planner book), 172
Lincoln, Abraham, 4
Linear *(chronos)* time, 114

Little Doer/Big Dreamer personality profile, 163
*Little Prince, The* (Saint-Exupéry), 8
Location for distribution planning, 113–14, 120
Logical (left brain)/creative (right brain), 97–98, **98,** 106, **107**
Logos, redesigning, 54–55
Lombardi, Vince, 17
Longfellow, Henry Wadsworth, 41
Loyalty programs for legacy, 83
Lucci, Susan, 120
Lundrum, Gene, 160

MacDonald, 1
Madonna, 57
Mage, Gene, 33
Mainwaring, Don, 61, 88
Majestic Athletic, 29
Making a difference, 77–78, **80**
Making your mark (second Wind of Life), 58
Marantz, xiii, 2
Market assessment, *xiii,* 13–26
    avoiding your strengths, 19
    building on your key strengths, 15–16
    competition analysis, 15, 16
    complementary capabilities, 18, 20, 158
    evaluating strengths and weaknesses, 13, 14–15, 16–17, **23–24**
    executive summary, 23
    exercises, **23–26**
    greatness, going for, 22–23, **25**
    identity card (new), 17, **26**
    importance of, 13–14, 23
    niche, finding your, 13–14
    passions and, 14, 17, 22
    personal snapshot, 16–17, 23, **24–25**
    real strengths, 18
    reflection on, 26
    "situation review," personal, 16–17, 23, **24–25**
    trends, recognizing, 16
    weaknesses, managing your, 19–20, 21, 22, **24–25,** 26
    Ye Olde Ben Franklin Chart, **24–25**
    *See also* Strengths; Target customer, identifying

Marketing Plan for Life, xi–xiv, xiii–xiv,
171–73, 175. *See also* Advertising
campaign, building; Business
you're in, defining;
Communication keys, hitting
your; Cycles, weathering;
Distribution, planning your;
Market assessment; Opportunity
targets, establishing; Profit and loss
analysis; Reach, expanding your;
Sales goals, achieving your;
Strategy, launching your; Target
customer, identifying
Marketing uniqueness
(communication key), 70, 71,
74–76, 78
Markova, Dawna, 4, 150
Masking the real you, 32–33, 36, **37**
Maslow, Abraham, 106
Mattel, 32
McCullough, David, 128
McDonald's, 40
McLuhan, Marshall, 81
McWilliams, Peter, 165
Mediums for legacy, 81–82, 89–90. *See
also* Reach, expanding your
Melville, Herman, 82
Membership programs for legacy,
83
Mental rehearsals, 129
Mentoring, personal legacy, 87–88, 90,
**91, 92**
Merck, 53–54
Mergers as opportunities, 158
Merrill, A. Roger, 114, 147–48
Merrill, Rebecca R., 114, 147–48
Michaels, Al, 160
Michelangelo, 105, 158
Michener, James, 162
Mini Cooper (BMW Group),
95–96
Miscellaneous goals, **137–38**
Mission statement, life strategy as, 40,
48
MLB Authentic Collection, 29
Monetary treadmill, 34
Montoya, Peter, 73–74
Morton, William, 6
Motorola, xiii, 61, 88
Multidimensional world and
uniqueness, 75

Munger, Charlie, 143
Mustang (Ford), 28

Name (communication key), 70, 71, **79**
Narrowcasting, 73–74, **79**
Nautilus, xiii
Negative energy, avoiding, 113
Net worth vs. self-worth, 150
New divisions as opportunities, 157
New identity card, 17, **26**
Newman, Paul, 87
Newman's Own, 87
New products and services as
opportunities, 156
New York Yankees, 15
Niche, finding your, 13–14. *See also*
Strategy, launching your
Nietzsche, Friedrich, 43
Nike, 39, 44–45
Nonaction vs. action, 43
Nordstrom, 72–73
Notre Dame, 157, 158
*Now, Discover Your Strengths*
(Buckingham and Clifton), 17

Oakland A's, 15
Objectives vs. goals, 126–27
Obsession vs. passion, 9
Office, The, 35
Ogilvy, David, 94
O'Neal, Shaquille, 18
*1,000 Marbles* (Davis), 120
Opportunity targets, establishing, *xiv,*
155–69
acquisitions as opportunities, 158
alliances as opportunities, 157–58
Big Dreamer/Little Doer
personality profile, 163
Chaos Commando personality
profile, 163
complementary capabilities, 18, 20,
158
courage to fulfill dreams, 164–65, 166
divisions (new) as opportunities, 157
doubters of dreams, 162–63, 166
Dream Maker personality profile,
164
dreams, **166–69**
executive summary, 165
exercises, **166–69**
importance of, 155–56, 165

impossible dreams, 159–61
licensing as opportunities, 159
mergers as opportunities, 158
partnerships as opportunities,
157–58
perseverance for, 161
personality profiles and dreams,
163–64
products and services (new) as
opportunities, 156
Realist personality profile, 164
realizing your dreams, **167**
reflection on, 169
regrets, avoiding, 165, 166, **167**
Rock of Gibraltar personality
profile, 163
strengths for, 159
"tunnel vision," 164
twenty-eighty theory, 157
unfulfilled dreams, **167**
value-added systems, creating new,
158
visualizing dreams, 161, 164, 166
writing dreams down, **166–67**
*Oprah Winfrey Show,* 161
Origin of legacy, **91–92**
Oscar Mayer, 96
O'Shaughnessy, Arthur, 54

Partnerships as opportunities, 157–58
P.A.S.S. (Professional Advocates for
Special Students), 57
Passages in life, 58–59
Passion importance for
business you're in, defining, 4, **7,**
8–9, **11**
market assessment, 14, 17, 22
Past, importance for perspective on
future, 64, **66–67**
Pasteur, Louis, 128, 131
Paul Masson, 114
*People Are Talking,* 160
Pepsi, 30
Pepsico, 89
Perceived value of specialization, 73
Perception (positive) importance, 71,
72–73
Perfection impact on
authenticity, 35
creativity, 98, 106, **108**
Perfect timing, 45, **49–50**

Perseverance for
    goals, 128–29, 132–33, **138**
    opportunities, 161
Personal balance sheet. *See* Profit and
    loss analysis
Personal brand building, 70–71, 72–74,
    78, **79, 80.** *See also*
    Communication keys, hitting
    your
Personal creation of a legacy, 84–88,
    90, **90–92**
Personal enrichment, 33–35
Personal growth goals, **136–37**
Personal integrity account, balancing,
    147–48, 151
Personality profiles and dreams,
    163–64
Personal reinvention, 56–58, 64, **67**
Personal snapshot, 16–17, 23, **24–25**
Personal vs. professional goals, 126
Philanthropy, 83, 86–87
*Philegatia: Living a Vision, Leaving a
    Legacy* (Young-Preston), 82
Picasso, Pablo, 93
Planet Inc., 77
Polaschek, Devon, 64
Positive energy, power of, 112–13
Post-It Notes (3M Company), 103
Powell, Colin, 72, 120
Powell, John, 75
Presentation dynamics element of
    advertising, 94, 100–101
Presley, Elvis, 4, 150
Pressure to create value, scandal from,
    141
Presumed expertise benefit of
    specialization, 73
Pretense, avoiding, 32, 36
Process, creativity as a, 101–2, 106
Procter & Gamble (P&G), 142
Product layering-on concept, 53, 54,
    55–56, 64
Products and services (new) as
    opportunities, 156
Product/service (communication key),
    70, 71, **79**
Professional Advocates for Special
    Students (P.A.S.S.), 57
Professional vs. personal goals, 126
Profit and loss analysis, *xiv,* 139–53
    aging and values, 146–47, **147**

appreciation in value, 149
balancing your personal integrity
    account, 147–48, 151
Berkshire Hathaway, 143–44
boomer generation and values,
    146–47
core values, identifying, 144–46,
    **144–46,** 148, 149, 150, 151, **151–53**
corporate failures, 139–40, 141
Depression-era and values, 146
executive summary, 151
exercises, **151–53**
forming your value system, 146–47,
    **147**
identifying core values, 144–46,
    **144–46,** 148, 149, 150, 151
importance of, 139–40, 151
integrity account (personal),
    balancing, 147–48, 151
Johnson & Johnson (J&J), 142–43
net worth vs. self-worth, 150
personal integrity account,
    balancing, 147–48, 151
pressure to create value, scandal
    from, 141
Procter & Gamble (P&G), 142
reflection on, 153
security from values, 150
self-worth/self-esteem, 150, **153**
sources of values, 147, **147**
value system, 140, 141, 142–50,
    **144–47,** 151, **151–53**
*See also* Opportunity targets,
    establishing
Psychographics for target customer,
    27–28, 36
*Psychology Today,* 64
Public announcement of goals,
    127
*Pumping Iron,* 56
Purpose, defining, 4–8, **7,** 9, **10**
*Purpose Driven Life, The* (Warren), 5,
    115, 150

Quaid, Dennis, 6
Quality *(kairos)* time, 114
Quality time with quality people,
    112–13, 114, 115, 119, 120
Quasar Electronics Company, xiii,
    100–101
Quindlen, Anna, 115, 118

Raising children, personal legacy,
    84–85, 90, **91**
Ralph Lauren, 159
Reach, expanding your, *xiii,* 81–92
    business creation of a legacy, 83–84,
    89–90
    "cause marketing," business legacy,
    84
    charitable contributions, business
    legacy, 83, 90
    charitable contributions, personal
    legacy, 86–87, 90, **91**
    children, personal legacy, 84–85, 90,
    **91**
    community programs, business
    legacy, 83, 90
    community programs, personal
    legacy, 86–87
    defining your legacy, **90**
    event marketing, business legacy, 83
    everyday good deeds, personal
    legacy, 88, 90, **92**
    executive summary, 89–90
    exercises, **90–92**
    fulfillment from, 82
    giving back for, 82, 83–84, 86–87, 90,
    **91**
    good deeds (everyday), personal
    legacy, 88, 90, **92**
    higher meaning, searching for,
    88–89, 90
    importance of, 81–82, 89–90
    improving lives of others by, 82,
    83–84, 85
    loyalty programs for, 83
    mediums for, 81–82, 89–90
    membership programs for, 83
    mentoring, personal legacy, 87–88,
    90, **91, 92**
    origin of legacy, **91–92**
    personal creation of a legacy, 84–88,
    90, **90–92**
    philanthropy, 83, 86–87
    raising children, personal legacy,
    84–85, 90, **91**
    reflection on, 92
    searching for a higher meaning,
    88–89, 90
    technological advances impact on,
    81–82
    traditional media for, 81

Reach (*cont.*)
    work, personal legacy, 85, 90, **91**
    *See also* Advertising campaign,
        building
Reach element of advertising, 94
Reaching out to make your personal
        goals a reality. *See* Profit and loss
        analysis
Reagan, Ronald, 56
Realist personality profile, 164
Realizing your dreams, **167**
Real life, getting a, 118–19
Real strengths, 18
Reavey, Ed, 61, 88
Reawakening your creative spirit, 100.
        *See also* Advertising campaign,
        building
Redefinition, constant, 2–4
Redstone, Sumner, 132
Reflection on
    advertising campaign, building, 109
    business you're in, defining, 11
    communication keys, hitting your, 80
    cycles, weathering, 67
    distribution, planning your, 124
    market assessment, 26
    opportunity targets, establishing, 169
    profit and loss analysis, 153
    reach, expanding your, 92
    sales goals, achieving your, 138
    strategy, launching your, 52
    target customer, identifying, 38
Regrets, avoiding, 165, 166, **167**
Reighard, Dwight ("Ike"), 30, 59
Reinventing yourself, 56–58, 64, **67**. *See
        also* Cycles, weathering
Relationship goals, **136**
Respecting your uniqueness, 76
Richards, Keith, xiv
Richardson, Cheryl, 150
Right brain (creative)/left brain
        (logical), 97–98, **98**, 106, **107**
Right risks, 46–47, 48
*Right Risk* (Treasurer), 46
Risk-taking, 39, 40, 41, 44–47, 48,
        **50–52**
Rituals for creativity, 102–3
Robbins, Tony, 72
Robinson, Jackie, 87
Robinson, Joe, 17
Robinson, Phil Alden, 85

Rock of Gibraltar personality profile,
        163
Roebling, Emily, 128
Roebling, John A., 128
Roebling, Washington, 128
*Rookie, The,* 6
Rooney, Andy, 119
Roosevelt, Eleanor, 161
Rosen, Jared, 149
Rousseau, Jean-Jacques, 103
Rubin, Harriet, 33, 35
Ruskin, John, 41
Ruth, Babe, 132

Saint-Exupéry, Antoine de, 8, 35, 88
Sales goals, achieving your, *xiv,* 125–38
    affirmations for, 127
    big, thinking, 131–32
    career/professional goals, **135**
    creative visualization, 105, 129
    daily affirmations for, 127
    executive summary, 133
    exercises, **134–38**
    failure, fear of, 132, 133, **138**
    family goals, **134**
    financial goals, **135–36**
    focusing on goals, 127
    goals vs. objectives, 126–27
    growth goals (personal), **136–37**
    health goals, **134–35**
    importance of, 125–26, 133
    leisure time and travel goals, **137**
    mental rehearsals, 129
    miscellaneous goals, **137–38**
    objectives vs. goals, 126–27
    perseverance for, 128–29, 132–33,
        **138**
    personal growth goals, **136–37**
    personal vs. professional goals, 126
    public announcement of goals, 127
    reflection on, 138
    relationship goals, **136**
    success, visualizing, 127, 129–31
    symbols of goals, 127
    thinking big, 131–32
    visible place for goals, 127
    visualizing success, 127, 129–31
    "what" of achieving goals, 126, 133
    "when" of achieving goals, 126, 133
    writing goals down, 127, **134–38**
    *See also* Profit and loss analysis

Salk, James, 105
Satisfaction with what you have, 33
*Scarlet Letter, The* (Hawthorne), 32
Scharf-Hunt, Diana, 125
*Schindler's List,* 86–87
Schwartz-Salant, Nathan, 35
Schwarzenegger, Arnold, 56
Scott, Julie Jordan, 5
Scott Newman Center, 87
Sculley, John, 89
Searching for a higher meaning, 88–89,
        90
Second Wind of Life (making your
        mark), 58
Security from values, 150
Self-discovery questions, **10–11**
Self-worth/self-esteem, 150, **153**
Seneca, 47
Seuss, Dr., 30
Shakespeare, William, 32, 35, 36
Sharapova, Maria, 165
Share of mind vs. share of market, 97
Sharing your time and energy wisely.
        *See* Distribution, planning your
Shaw, George Bernard, 165
Shuker, Scott, 82
Simplicity for authenticity, 30–31, **38**
Simpson, Alan, 149
Sinatra, Frank, 112
"Situation review," personal, 16–17, 23,
        **24–25**
Smith, Fred, 131–32
Snapshot (personal), 16–17, 23, **24–25**
Soaring Oaks Consulting, 33
Sources of values, 147, **147**
Southwest Airlines, 73
Spears, Britney, 74
Specialization, 73–74, **79**
Spending time wisely, 115–16, 157
Sperry, Roger W., 97
Spielberg, Steven, 86, 161
Starbucks, 157
Stedman, Allen, 77
Stevenson, Robert Louis, 35
Stewart, Jimmy, 88
Strategy, launching your, *xiii,* 39–52
    action for, 39–40, 41–44, 47–48, **48–49**
    calculated risks, 44
    call to action for, 39–40, 41–44,
        47–48, **48–49**
    courage for risk-taking, 47, 48

discomfort, leading to action, 43–44
executive summary, 47–48
exercises, **48–52**
fear of committing to action, 45
importance of, 39–40, 47–48
inaction, society plagued with, 42
mission statement, life strategy as, 40, 48
nonaction vs. action, 43
perfect timing, 45, **49–50**
reflection on, 52
right risks, 46–47, 48
risk-taking, 39, 40, 41, 44–47, 48, **50–52**
taking the leap, 45–46, **48–49**
unique competence for, 39, 40–41
words vs. actions, 42–43
*See also* Cycles, weathering
Streisand, Barbra, 162
Strengths
avoiding your, 19
capitalizing on your, 13, 15–16, **25**
defined, 14
evaluating, 13, 14–15, 16–17, **23–24**
opportunity targets and, 159
specialization benefit, 73
weakness, strength as, 20, 21
*See also* Market assessment
Success
defined, xi–xii
visualizing, 127, 129–31
*See also* Marketing Plan for Life
Survivors of the Shoah Visual History Foundation, 86–87
Swift, Jonathan, 105
Symbols of goals, 127
Szent-Györgyi, Albert von, 103

Taking the leap, 45–46, **48–49**
*Tales of the South Pacific* (Michener), 162
Tallying your personal balance sheet. *See* Profit and loss analysis
Target customer, identifying, *xiii*, 27–38
authenticity as key for, 29–30, 32, 35–36, **37–38**
backward, living our lives, 34–35
being true to yourself, 30
choices, authentic, 35

demographics for, 27–28, 36
"Easterlin Paradox," 34
enoughness concept, 34
enrichment (personal), 33–35
exercises, **37–38**
happiness, 33–35
honesty for authenticity, 36
hypocrisy, avoiding, 32, 36
importance of, 27–28, 36
"Influentials," 34
less is more, 31, **38**
masking the real you, 32–33, 36, **37**
monetary treadmill, 34
perfection, 35
personal enrichment, 33–35
pretense, avoiding, 32, 36
psychographics for, 27–28, 36
reflection on, 38
satisfaction with what you have, 33
simplicity for, 30–31, **38**
true to yourself, being, 30
"United States of Anxiety," 33
*See also* Strategy, launching your
Targets of opportunity. *See* Opportunity targets, establishing
*Technique for Producing Ideas, A* (Young), 101
Technological advances impact on legacy, 81–82
Terminal illness, thinking of life as, 118
Thinking big, 131–32
Third Wind, 172, 173
Third Wind of Life (discovery), 58–59
3M Company, 103
Three Winds of Life, 58–59
Time, distributing wisely, **121**. *See also* Distribution, planning your
"Time off," gift of, 119
Timing for distribution planning, 114
Top-of-mind vs. back-of-mind awareness, 97
Traditional media for legacy, 81
Treasurer, Bill, 32, 35, 46–47
Trends, recognizing, 16
"True north" (purpose), defining, 4–8, **7**, 9, **10**
True to yourself, being, 30
Trust, building, 72–73
Tsongas, Paul, 115
"Tunnel vision," 164

Turner, Ted, 131
Twain, Mark, 141, 166
Twelve-Point Marketing Plan, *xiii–xiv*, 61, 88. *See also* Marketing Plan for Life
Twenty-eighty theory, 157
*Twins,* 56
Tyco, 140

Understandability benefit of specialization, 73
Unfinished business and defining purpose in life, 4
Unfulfilled dreams, **167**
Unhappiness, 9
Unique competence for strategy, 39, 40–41
Uniqueness of marketing (communication key), 70, 71, 74–76, 78
United Airlines, 157
United Parcel Service (UPS), 3
"United States of Anxiety," 33
University of Minnesota, 157, 158
*Unstoppable* (Kersey), 6, 132
U.S. Olympic Hockey Team, 159–60

Vacations, gift of, 119
Value-added systems, creating new, 158
Value (perceived) of specialization, 73
Value system, 140, 141, 142–50, **144–47**, 151, **151–53**
Vandehey, Tim, 73–74
Vinci, Leonardo da, 99
Visible place for goals, 127
Vision element of advertising, 94, 105, **109**
Visualizing
dreams, 161, 164, 166
success, 127, 129–31
Volkswagen, 97

Wallace, William, 47
Walt Disney Company, 156
Warner, Kurt, 131
Warren, Rick, 5, 115, 116, 150
Weaknesses, managing your, 19–20, 21, 22, **24–25, 26**
Welles, Orson, 114
Wendy's, 40–41

*What Happy People Know* (Baker), 34, 115

"What" of achieving goals, 126, 133

*What Should I Do with My Life?* (Bronson), 5, 89

"When" of achieving goals, 126, 133

"Whispering campaign," 96

Williams, Serena, 165

Wilson, Woodrow, 89

Winds of Life, 58–59

Winfrey, Oprah, 160–61

Word of mouth advertising, 96

Words vs. actions, 42–43

Work, personal legacy, 85, 90, **91**

Workspace (personal) for creativity, 104

*Work To Live* (Robinson), 17

WorldCom, 140, 141

Wozniak, Steve, 162

Writing down
dreams, **166–67**
goals, 127, **134–38**

Yanagaswa, Dr., 60

Ye Olde Ben Franklin Chart, **24–25**

Young, James Webb, 101, 102

Young, Margaret, 34–35

Young-Preston, Glenn E., 82

Ziglar, Zig, 2–3

Zimmerman, Stuart, 149

Zoglio, Suzanne, 36

Marketing strategist Robert Fried has spent most of his career directing or repositioning the marketing and sales strategies of blue-chip Fortune 500 companies. He has been the chief marketing executive for companies including Motorola, Quasar Electronics, Marantz Stereo, Nautilus Fitness, and Hansen's Juice and Soda. He is the founder of BrandMark, Inc., a marketing consulting firm with several high-profile international clients.

Fried codified the 12-Point Marketing Plan process that offers companies of all sizes step-by-step brand marketing solutions. He later created a work/life seminar series called "A Marketing Plan for Life" utilizing the same marketing planning process. These seminars have been conducted around the world, including a presentation to guests at the world renowned Canyon Ranch Resort, and an international symposium of sales executives in Milan, Italy.

Fried is the cofounder of the Third Wind Company, which was created to encourage, motivate, and inspire people to take action to discover what really matters most to them. He has been a frequent guest lecturer on many major college campuses including UCLA's Anderson School of Business and USC's Marshall School of Business.